Matthew Boulton College

RECONSTRUCTING THE BLACK IMAGE

Gordon de la Mothe

t6

Trentham Books

First published in 1993 by Trentham Books Limited

Trentham Books Limited
Westview House
734 London Road
Oakhill
Stoke-on-Trent
Staffordshire
England ST4 5NP

© Gordon de la Mothe

British Library Cataloguing Publication Data
Mothe, Gordon De La
    Reconstructing the Black Image
    I. Title
    704.942

    ISBN: 0 948080 61 2

Cover: '*Battle between Heraclius and Chosroes*' fresco by Piero della
Francesca in the Chruch of San Francesco in Arezzo.

Designed and typeset by Trentham Print Design Limited
and printed by Bemrose Shafron Limited, Chester.

Contents

The Genesis of This Book

I arrived in Britain in July 1958, three weeks before the Notting Hill Riots, and for me the experiences of the time were traumatic. Two years later my wife and young family joined me and we struggled to survive. By 1964 I realised that surviving as an itinerant, semi-skilled worker offered little hope for the future and I began to attend the nearby College of Art and Technology at Luton, Bedfordshire, as a part-time student, working full-time assembling cars at Vauxhall Motors. After three years I became a full-time student on the Art Foundation course and followed through to a Diploma in Art and Design (Fine Art) at Maidstone and an Art Teachers Diploma at Liverpool.

I began teaching in Kent, having moved my family there while I was studying at Maidstone. My spare time activity was painting, and between 1974 and 1980 I exhibited my work at several venues in London and the South East, and twice in each of the Royal Academy Summer Exhibition, the Royal Society of British Artists and the New English Art Society. I also exhibited in the *Drum Magazine* Afro-Caribbean Exhibition at Covent Garden in 1976 and, later, became a founder member of The Rainbow Art Group which functioned for a while as the Visual Arts wing of the Minority Arts Advisory Service — when it served 'the arts that Britain ignores'.

In 1979 I joined the Caribbean Teachers Association which was actively trying to effect changes in Britain that would accommodate the presence of people from the New Commonwealth within the society. It had been clear to many West Indian parents that there was something wrong with the British educational system, as far as their children were concerned but it was Bernard Coard's book of 1941, *How the West Indian Child is Made Educationally Sub-normal in the British School System* that brought the matter to public notice. The Government finally tried to address this matter by setting up a committee of inquiry, chaired initially by Rampton and then by Swann.

The CTA was then in the process of setting up its own Supplementary School (now the Robert Hart Memorial Supplementary School) in Peckham and

vii

Counselling Project. The late Bob Hart was Secretary of the organisation and Trevor Carter, no longer Chairman, was very active in his support. At a conference held at Hornsey Town Hall in March 1980, to discuss the organisation's co-operation with the Rampton Committee, an appeal was made for members to do what they could within their subject areas to help pupils to gain more positive views of themselves, and I pondered as to what could be done by an Art teacher based in Maidstone.

At Liverpool I had written a thesis on the mixed-race population which I called 'The Victims of Myths'. It contained a comparative study of the conditions of slaves in the Caribbean and those of the British working class of the same period. I had been advised by Ilene Melish, then at the Sociology Department at Liverpool University, that the sections of the work should be developed and published. But I felt it was time for family needs to take precedence at last, and the work was shelved.

When I looked at the work again, I decided that it had to have visual appeal and began to collect images on slides and as photocopies. I scanned all European art before the sixteenth century for images of black people and began to arrange them in chronological order. This set me reading work by researchers such as J.A. Rogers, Kenneth Little and Edward Scobie. I took resultant documentation and slides to Bob Hart. The package fitted in with his plans for leadership conferences for young people of 14-16 from several schools in Southwark.

I was to set the tone of these Saturday conferences at the Commonwealth Institute with an illustrated lecture on 'Black Images in the History of Art'. The impact of my first presentation — on students, their teachers, and ILEA's Inspector for Multi-ethnic Education in 1980 was tremendous. The Inspector regularly attended these conferences, and later invited me to lecture on courses for teachers.

Having to do these lectures made me painfully aware of my own limitations and set me on a course of self-education. My search for images intensified, and I began to discover the joy in finding very relevant images in unexpected places. This had to be supported by extensive reading, so I read and read. Many of the authors listed in the bibliography became my constant companions, and for a time my wife and family again took second place, this time to my new-found literary friends. I cannot thank my family enough for their tolerance and understanding during my period of obsession, as I struggled to make sense of what I was seeing and learning, and then tried to fit that information into my own perceptions. The course of my life changed and, although I still paint occasionally, painting took second place to the fascinating research.

For many years I received a considerable amount of lip-service and offers of assistance in getting the work published but nothing materialised.

It dawned on me that my amateur approach to scholarship and my communal attitude to life had made me an exploitable resource for others who were more career-minded, academically certificated and employed in positions of authority.

In 1985 I moved to London. Gus John suggested that I show my work to Alan Murray at the Further Education Unit of the Department of Education and Science. Alan thought that the material would be more accessible to pupils if divided into sections rather than in one historical sequence, so inspiring the present form of the work. He commissioned it as a project named 'Black images and Identity for the 16-19 Curriculum' RP373. It was completed and approved in 1987. However, problems arose with some of my work associates, and Alan left the FEU. Difficulties arose over the format of the proposed publication related to its cost and, despite an appeal to the ILEA in its last months, the material was not published and the FEU released the copyright to me.

Alan suggested that I contact Gillian Klein and we eventually met. Gillian's response was enthusiastic and she has contributed to the work by her judicious editing, for which I am truly thankful. Other individuals who have given me encouragement and support include Len Garrison of The African Peoples Historical Foundation (UK); Ronny Clarke of the Sojourner Truth Youth Association and O. M. Gibbs, former Higher Commissioner for Grenada. I would also like to thank the Jamaican High Commission for the information they provided on the history of the island.

Reconstructing the Black Image

A guide for users

This book aims to develop curriculum approaches and material appropriate to black students which would enhance their personal development, self esteem, competence and understanding of society, and also enable young people from the white community to develop core competences, and a greater understanding of the contributions made by black people to history and social development.

Images have been used as stimuli; the social and historical realities relating to images are linked here to produce a thesis as a point of departure for further study and research.

This thesis does not present alternative facts. It offers a view of known facts which questions many of the attitudes currently held in society. It takes into account relevant related knowledge which is often neglected or treated as insignificant within the education system, and sets it within a multicultural context.

Supporting material is provided for the first two sections, to encourage a greater understanding of the areas which they select for further study. It is expected that they should develop an awareness of relevant material which they encounter in their daily lives and in the pursuit of other fields of activity. This may apply to teachers who find that they are encountering areas in which their knowledge is limited.

The material ranges across time, geographical barriers and areas of discipline, offering an open-ended view to the curriculum, from which teachers can adapt and select as appropriate.

1

SECTION ONE

White history and the distortion of black history

Image I.1 — Bronze from Benin

A Bronze cast portrait from the Court of the Oba of Benin. Many such objects of art — the most elaborate and advanced art works to come out of Africa — were looted when the British sent a military expedition to Benin in 1897.

For many decades European scholars have projected the idea that these works had been influenced by the Portuguese.[1]

Image I.2 — Nok Terracotta

However, mining operations near the village of Nok earlier this century have uncovered many objects made from terracotta which had been buried for a long time. The style and quality of these works have established that the Bronzes of Benin had their origins in the more remote past of the people of the area, as carbon dating has placed the culture which produced these works into the period 700 B.C. to 200 A.D.[2]

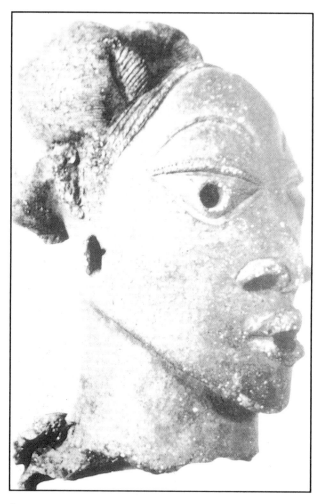

Image I.3 — Adoration of The Magi

There is a long-accepted tradition of depicting a black King among the Three Wise Men who visited the infant Jesus. This provides a clue to the position of African people, and their descendants, living in the West and demands a reassessment of their status. In many European paintings, right up to the 16th century, The black Magus is shown in costumes more richly adorned than those of the other two magi.

Image I.4 — Cresques Map of Europe and West Africa

This tradition may have been inspired by the famous pilgrimage of Mansa Musa to Mecca in 1324 A.D.

Mansa Musa was the King of Mali and was considered the wealthiest monarch in the world at the time. During his famous pilgrimage he distributed so much gold, in trade and gifts, that the price of gold on the general market fell and did not recover for about twelve years.[3]

This map by Abraham Cresques shows the King and the 'GOLDEN ROAD TO EGYPT', from where the gold of West Africa was distributed to the world markets.

Image I.5 — Tortured Indian

The 'discovery' of America and the large quantities of gold possessed by the native Americans, reduced the importance of the African gold trade to Europe. Whereas Columbus first wrote of the Indians as a simple, friendly people who would make good Christians, those who followed him abused and tortured them to produce gold and later to work on the plantations when sugar was introduced to the area.[4]

I. 6 — Indians with no Heads

In order to justify their treatment of the Indians, the Spanish settlers projected an image of the Indians as cruel, cannibalistic and monstrous, sometimes with faces like dogs' or even with no heads at all, portraying their faces on their chests. Many priests tried to save the Indians and attempted to convert them to Christianity, but settlers and officials objected, on grounds that they were animals and might not even have souls.[5]

The Vatican finally decided that the Indians had souls after all, but by then the idea had caught on that African people might be better than Indians for working on the plantations, so slaves were sought in Africa.

I. 7 — Visitors to the African Continent

The European traders who first went to Africa met established societies with well defined customs, practices and beliefs, and the traders had to behave, in the presence of the African Rulers, in much the same manner as they would have done with rulers in Europe.[6] The African societies of the coast of Africa were so well established that they controlled the trade in goods and slaves from the interior and the Europeans knew little of what existed beyond the coastline.

I. 8 — Descilers Map

The Descilers Map of 1550 shows the Nile flowing from as far south as Zimbabwe and the location of the Kingdom of Prester John in the Horn of Africa. This mythical King was supposed to have gone from Europe to Africa and the East — and created an ideal Christian Kingdom. The map also shows headless men and men with several pairs of arms, living in the interior.[7]

By permission of the British Library

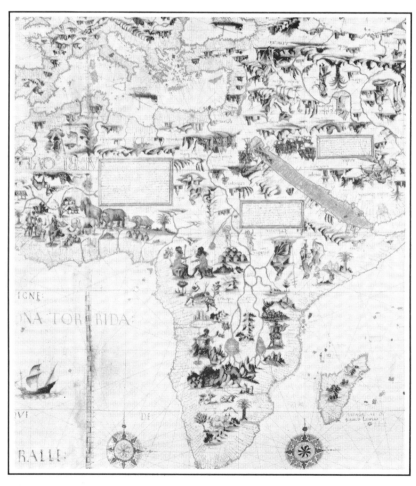

I. 9 — Slave Traders on the Coast

As time went on, the European traders began to demand more and more slaves in return for their goods, amongst which were firearms, which they would sell only to African rulers who provided them with slaves.[8]

By these and other methods the trade in slaves increased and so did the incidence of tribal warfare and cruelty.

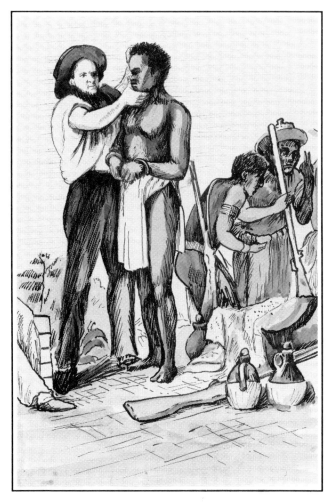

I. 10 — Ship Burned by Slaves

Those taken into slavery did not go willingly. It was necessary to chain them and lock them up in confined spaces, because they were known to try to escape by attacking the crews of the slave ships, jumping overboard and even setting fire to the ships. The slave trade is now part of the history of the West and its effects are still with us. Three hundred years of enslavement of its people have led to the formulation of a debased view of Africa and its people in the minds of Europeans.

I. 11 — Modern Blacks doing Menial Work

Disparaging and demeaning portrayals of black people served the political and social purposes first of justifying their enslavement and, once slavery was abolished, confirming that black people were suited only to low status and the performing of menial tasks. In the light of those perceptions, the art works of Benin can now be recognised as one reminder of the independent past of Africa and of the ability of the African people to create societies and art forms of their own.

I. 12 — Rhodesian Poster 1938

This poster, produced by the colonists of Rhodesia in 1938, illustrates the settlers' notion that the African people could not create anything significant on their own.[9]

The stone structures of Great Zimbabwe, from which the modern country takes its name, were supposed to be not the work of African people but the creation of people from abroad — either Jewish followers of the Queen of Sheba or the Phoenicians, who had been sent around Africa by the Egyptians Pharaoh, Necho.

If we are to correct such false ideas of black people, based on centuries of distorted and demeaning images, but still current, we need to learn about the history and creations of the people of Africa prior to the Europeans' slave trade and their colonisation of the continent.

A 1938 Rhodesian poster; a black offers gold to a spectral queen of Sheba

SECTION ONE

SECTION ONE

White History and the distortion of Black History

Teachers' Notes

The Historical Context

Since the end of World War II, the presence of black people in Europe, their struggles for their rights in the Western World and the struggles of Africans to gain their independence from their colonial masters, have been important aspects of the changing pattern of world events. The period of political colonisation has ended and the colonisers have to adjust to the new realities of the modern world.

Changes Brought About by the Discovery of The New World

In the middle of this century, Timbuktu, once the capital of the kingdom of Mali, was considered remote and inaccessible. Today, Timbuktu is no longer considered quite so remote but the area called Mali, which forms only part of the earlier kingdom, is not known for its wealth. Its claim to world attention is that it is an area prone to drought, poverty and starvation. Few people in the West are aware that it was once part of a wealthy and influential kingdom.

In many ways, the fate of Mali reflects the way that modern history has affected African people and their descendants throughout the world. A people once rated among the wealthiest in the world, with their own beliefs, forms of social organisation and culture, have been debased; first by a period when many of their numbers were forced into a unique form of slavery, and then by the colonisation of their continent by the people of another, whose present position of wealth and power was, and is, in part the product of that slavery.

European expansion in the 15th century followed the pattern of exploration, colonisation and exploitation.

The knights of Europe were given a double incentive, by the Pope and by their immediate rulers: all their sins, past, present and future, would be forgiven by God, if they went out and fought in His name, and they would be allowed to keep part of the goods they plundered. In time, this custom of plundering the property of the Muslims was extended to all other unbelievers. So much so, that Queen Elizabeth sent seamen on voyages of discovery with instructions to 'seize all land that does not belong to a Christian King'.

The Caribs and other Indians of The New World

The 'discovery' of the New World, with its large quantities of gold, was first exploited by the Spaniards. When they found that they needed the knowledge and labour of the Indian population, they forced them into slavery and tortured them into obedience. Many however, killed themselves rather than be taken captive.

To justify their treatment of the natives, the Europeans promoted a view of the Indians as inferior beings, more animal than human and possibly even without souls. The Pope and the Cardinals of Rome debated for years about whether or not the Indians had souls. While the debate went on, profits made at the expense of heathen lives became more important than the possibility of bringing their souls to God. The dehumanising of non-Europeans had begun.

The first group of Indians encountered by the Spaniards on arrival in the New World were the Arawaks of the Northern Caribbean Islands.[10] The Arawaks wore gold ornaments and this excited Spanish greed. The Spaniards came without women and took native women when and as they pleased. The Arawaks were not a warlike people and their arms were no match for those of the Spaniards. Within one hundred and fifty years, the Arawaks were exterminated.

Many of the early settlers had been soldiers who had fought against the Moors in Spain. They were skilled in the use of arms and used to taking the life of non-christians. Others were criminals who had been banished. The soldiers were not accustomed to providing for themselves and used force to make the Arawaks provide them with food and gold. They modelled themselves on the Hidalgo system of the land-owning nobles of Spain and, adapting their class attitudes, used the Arawaks as manual labourers and even hunted them for sport.

The priests who accompanied the settlers did not comply with the instructions of the Papal Bull of May 1493 which stated that the inhabitants of the Americas should be instructed in the Catholic faith. Nor did they insist that the Spanish settlers adhere to the Ten Commandments.

By 1495 Columbus and Alonso de Ojeda began killing the Arawaks of the Cibas and Vega Real districts of Hispaniola. Avando completed the extermination of the Tanios — another Indian group — in 1503. Bloodhounds were used to hunt Indians down and tear them to pieces and others were murdered in cold blood as the former soldiers practiced their military skills, taking bets among themselves on who could strike off the head of an Indian with a single blow.[11]

In her book *Sex in History,* Reay Tannahil describes how, in the cannabalist Caribs and the Aztecs who practiced human sacrifice, the Spaniards found the perfect excuse for their behaviour. By the time that the case for the protection of the Indians was brought before the Vatican Council, it was the behaviour of the Indians which was held up to judgement. The collective evils of all the tribes was attributed to every Indian: they were cannibals, practiced human sacrifice, sodomy, incest, adultery, drug-abuse, drunkenness, robbery and murder.

The only sin they were not accused of was heresy, since they could not be pagans and heretics at the same time. They were judged by the Europeans to be highly irrational (or non-rational), no better than the brute beast. Assuming the convenient ideology that 'irrational creatures cannot have dominion... because dominion signified rights... since irrational creatures cannot have rights it follows that they cannot have dominion', the Spaniards claimed that they were entitled to all that belonged to the Indians.

When Pope Paul III ruled that the Indians were 'truly men', his ruling was dismissed as 'biased' by the exponents of the 'irrational' ideology, and the abuse of the Indians continued. Some religious men joined in: such as Archbishop Zumarraga in Mexico and Bishop Landa in Yucatan, who seized all the religious and legal records of the Indians and burned them. In this way many of the records of the pre-Columbian period were destroyed.

The 'discovery' of the New World by Europeans, the seizure of gold and precious metals from the Indians, and the later development of agriculture, in particular the production of sugar, resulted in a shift in both the trade and the location of the important trading ports of Europe, from those of Italy and

Southern France to those of Spain, Portugal, France, England and Holland. The important trade routes had shifted from across the Mediterranean to across the Atlantic. The northern coast of Africa lost much of its importance. The north-west was by-passed, as ships from Spain and Portugal and, later, England, France and Holland made their way to the West coast. Then they sailed south down the coast. From there they made their way to Central America and then back to their home ports, so completing the 'triangular trade', which brought great wealth to Europe.

The Introduction of African Slaves

The first African slaves were brought to the Caribbean in 1502.[12] They had been converted to Christianity in Spain, where they performed such tasks as their abilities allowed; some were put to administration or to skilled trades, and marriage to native Spanish women was encouraged.

The Africans brought to the Caribbean worked alongside the Indian slaves in the sugar industry, introduced to the area by the Spaniards. It was noticed that they survived, while the Indians died or killed themselves. In the hope of saving the Indians from extermination, many priests tried to get better treatment for the Indians. Among them was Bartolome de la Casas, who suggested that African slaves might prove to be tougher and more resilient. In 1518 King Charles V of Spain granted a license for the supply of '4000 African slaves to Hispaniola'.

So began the physical abuse and character assassination of an entire people, and the negative portrayal of all things African. Until 1550 the Descilers map depicted the continent much as we know it today. Whereas the De Moras Map of 1761 asserts that:

> It is true that the centre of the continent is filled with burning sand, savage beasts, and almost uninhabitable deserts. The scarcity of water forces the different animals to come together to the same place for drinking. Finding themselves together at a time when they are in heat, they have intercourse with one another without paying regard to the differences between species. Thus are produced those monsters which are found their in greater numbers than in any other part of the world.[13]

Added to the justification that had been used for the abuse of the Indians: that they were such primitive and cruel people that they did not even have souls, was the depiction of the frightful physical conditions under which the Africans were purported to live in their native land. Compared to these, slavery in the New World was a welcome release; and the possible saving of their souls — if souls they had — from evil and unnatural practices of which even the animals of their continent were not innocent.

In the 300 years during which the slave trade developed, the attitudes of Europeans towards Africans underwent several important changes. The system set up by the early European traders, by which they would trade only with African rulers, who were prepared to supply them with slaves and to whom they would in turn supply guns, resulted in the trade becoming widespread. Not to trade in slaves meant having no guns to resist those who did, and increased the possibility of being enslaved.[14] This became such established practice that in the later years it seemed that the Africans had always behaved in that way.

The past glories of Africa were forgotten, submerged under the weight of the slave trade. By the time the trade came to an end, the exploration and colonisation of Africa had began. The ravages caused by the trade were seen as the 'normal' condition of Africa and its people, not as the disaster it was to the continent.

Demeaning representations of black people

The slave trade came to an end because of a shift in power away from those who benefited directly from it, to those who saw it as an evil and degrading form of commerce. Rivalry between the European nations and between different forms of trade within countries had resulted in the sugar trade, which had the greatest need for slaves — particularly to the British Caribbean planters — losing its importance, so making the plantations unprofitable.

The process was a gradual one, and those who still for a time profited, resisted the move to abolition. One way of doing so was to enhance those ideas which had justified the trade, by applying concepts of pseudo-science, to 'prove' that the power and position acquired by Europeans was a natural outcome of superior intellect. Physical characteristics which differentiated white European masters from their black African slaves were focused upon and represented in a manner which assumed or seemed to endorse the asserted innate superiority of Europeans.[15] It was the time of the industrial revolution so the ability to manufacture goods and to produce works of art was put forward as proof of superiority. Slaves who had for many generations been relegated to menial and manual labour, were assumed to be incapable of mental and creative activity.[16] As further justifica-

tion, their relatives in Africa were declared to be primitive, naked savages, similarly incapable of creativity.

To create the right conditions for such ideas, it was convenient to forget the known contributions of black people to human development, as well as black societies, works of art and manufactured artefacts. Note for example how the ancient kingdoms of Ghana and Mali have been neglected in European records until recent times, or the way in which the re-discovery of Egypt was greeted by Europeans after Napoleon's invasion of that country, a mental and emotional barrier being put around its inland borders, separating it from the rest of Africa, with which it was said to have had little contact or relationship; note also how the records of early contacts and equal trading with Africans were 'forgotten' and where the ravages caused by one set of Europeans are later regarded by another group as the normal condition of Africans. Such as, on the Eastern coast of Africa, where the damage done by the Portuguese in the 16th century, was later seen as a normal way of life by the British in the 19th century.[17]

The buildings which had housed the splendour of Mutota, recorded by the Portuguese, were to become regarded as mysterious stone structures by the British settlers, who refused to accept the possibility that they could have been built by the native Africans. The new settlers therefore attributed the construction of Great Zimbabwe to the Queen of Sheba, or Arab traders. By then, Europeans held the power to define and explain facts and events, in terms which supported their own supposed superiority and the supposed inferiority of Africans and other black people throughout the world.

In 1897 the British government sent a punitive expedition to overthrow the Oba of Benin and his palace was looted of its collection of bronze art. Over two thousand pieces were taken away and floated on the art markets of Europe. In the custom of the time, the production of these works was attributed to foreign influences; in this case the Portuguese, who had traded with Benin in the sixteenth and seventeenth centuries and whose images appeared in some of the works. Europeans convinced themselves that Africans were incapable of creating anything requiring intelligence, skill and artistry, and for many years the foreign influence was accepted as the genius of the works. — (Source: *Prehistoric and Primitive Man* by Andreas Lommel, Paul Hamlyn 1966 p164).

Excavations earlier this century, however, revealed many terracotta images, which point to the earlier history of the region and its contact with the ancient world of the Mediterranean. This important discovery was made public in a publication by William Fagg in 1951. What is emerging from studies undertaken since, is that the contacts between West Africa and the ancient cultures were more extensive than previously believed. Far from being remote, uncivilised and pagan, Africa south of the Sahara had been contributing enormously to ancient civilisation. The incursion of Asian Muslims, who introduced a new element into the earlier Eurafrican culture, had effectively sealed off Africa from Europe for about eight hundred years.

During that time much had changed. The Crusades and their aftermath had created a divide, with European Christians on the southern shores of the Mediterranean and Muslim Afro-Asians on the northern shores of Africa. In time Europeans came to believe that only they were Christian and superior to the rest of the heathen/pagan world. In documents relating to the Crusades, it is quite common to find the execution of infidels described as 'slaughtering the heathen cattle'.

These ideas and attitudes greatly influenced European attitudes to the Indians of the New World during and after the voyages of Columbus, and the West African slave trade which came after. This was often justified on the grounds that Africans (like Indians) were inferior beings of lower intelligence who had made no contribution to human development. This false assumption, — still with us today — has clouded European perceptions of Africans, their history and their capabilities as human beings, for several hundred years.

What is now emerging is the reality that the African States south of the Sahara were within the catchment area of Egyptian, ancient classical and early Christen-Byzantine culture and had radiated a powerful creative influence[18]. Cut off by the Muslim incursion, the artistic influence were nurtured and preserved by the Yoruba tribe and had flowered first at Ife and then at Benin. But knowledge of this had not reached Europeans. Coming onto the European art market, the looted bronzes of Benin were silent testimonies against the long-held myth that Africans were incapable of high creative achievement and helped to bring other negative perceptions of Africa into question.

Developments and changes

In the 20th century, several events have enabled black people to increase efforts to change their situation. Two World Wars, in which black people have been involved either as volunteers or through coercion, have resulted in Black people travelling around the world as never before. Areas of Africa and the colonial empires have gained political independence, though often still economically dependent upon and exploited through trade by their former colonisers. In the West, black people still find themselves in inferior circumstances, materially poorer than their White neighbours, often unemployed or in menial positions in the labour force, and generally having to struggle continuously to assert their rights and maintain their dignity as human beings.

The African Past

Africa is now generally acknowledged to be the cradle of mankind. To the ancients, Egypt was not separated from the rest of the continent by an emotional wall but, with Nubia, constituted the Nile Valley civilisation. Situated on the north- eastern corner of the continent, it was well placed for contact with the civilisations of Mesopotamia, India, the Middle East and Southern Europe. The development of urban civilisations in Africa, Asia and Europe occurred in the regions where each was closest to one of the others. This suggests that such developments are likely to have been sparked off by foreign contacts and interaction.

The ancient monuments of the Nile Valley civilisation show that the population included a high proportion of black Africans and people with African ancestry. Many modern scholars now believe that until the Hyksos invasion, the Egyptian Pharaohs were all wholly or partly of African stock, as were the Pharaohs of the 18th Dynasty and again of the 25th.(Source: *Egypt the Black Land* by Paul Jordan.)

Nubia was closely associated with the more dominant and powerful Egypt. From the 3rd millennium BC, the Egyptians raided their southern black neighbours, driving off their herds of cattle, taking slaves and extracting tribute. In time an amicable relationship developed, and ultimately a high degree of interdependence.

Nubians served as Court Officials, soldiers and Tax Collectors in Egypt.[20] Many Egyptian priests were known to have Nubian wives[21], and as the practice of religious observance was hereditary, many, if not at all, of the priesthood was black. It was from this tradition that the story told by the Greek historian, Herodotus, of two black priestesses from the Temple being stolen and sold at Delphi and Dodona, where they were responsible for setting up the famous oracles, originated. Nubian girls were also popular as dancers, as evident on many Egyptian monuments.

The Triumph of Nubia

In about 1100 BC, Nubia established its independence from Egypt, and for several centuries existed as a separate Kingdom. In 750 BC, Nubia attacked and overcame the Egyptians and established the 25th Dynasty, which lasted until the Assyrian invasion in 665BC.[22]

Retreating southwards, the Nubians set up their capital at Napata. Later they moved to Meroe, where they established trade with Persia, Southern Arabia and India. Their industries included the production of iron goods, and in time they developed an original form of writing.

Nubia was overcome by the state of Axum which had developed to the south. Later there were influences brought in by Christianity, before the Islamic faith spread across the area.[23]

The Eastern Trading Ports

South of Nubia, trade had gone on for several centuries at many ports along the Eastern Coast of Africa, as far down as modern Mozambique. An Alexandrian pilot book: *The Peripulus of the Erythrean* published in 110 AD gives details of towns from the Red Sea to Mozambique. It lists the markets and ports of call, broken into daily runs: the people encountered, the goods to be bought and sold, the prevailing winds at different seasons. The towns flourished to the end of the 15th century. They included Lamu, Malindi, Pemba, Kilwa, Sofala, Zanzibar and Mombasa, and Swahili was the common language[24]. Their trade extended across the Indian Ocean to India, China and Malaya.

In the 16th century, the Portuguese looted and plundered most of the towns and attempted to control the trade, but were only partially successful. Ultimately they surrendered most of the town to the Swahili-speaking natives, but established a colony in Mozambique[25].

Great Zimbabwe

Gold had been an important commodity of the trade in the Eastern ports. We find in a book called *The Meadows of Gold and Mines of Gems*[26] by the Arab geographer Masudi in the tenth century, the first record of this trade. According to Masudi, the gold came from inland to the port of Sofala, just south of the Zambisi River. The area was later controlled by the Shona people, who in turn were superseded by the Rozwi, a branch of the Baranga people.

It was the Rozwi who built the stone structures which were for many decades the subject of fanciful speculations by Europeans. When the Portuguese arrived in the sixteenth century, the Rowzi controlled a large empire in that area, which the Arab traders called *I Mu'anamutapah*. The Portuguese corrupted this to Manamutapa in their records. (Source: *Discovery of Lost Worlds* by Magnus Magnusson, American Heritage Publishing, New York, *p102*.)

The empire was too large to be governed from a single base and was divided into provinces, governed by relatives of the King. When King Matope died, rivalries developed and the Portuguese manipulated these to their benefit, often taking sides and active roles in military interventions. In time, mining rights were demanded for their military services and a vassal King was installed in 1629,[27] who was forced to grant all mining rights to the Portuguese, as well as the right to expel the Arab and Swhali traders- collectively called 'Moors' by the Portuguese. The behaviour of settlers was such that Manoel Barreto, in a report to the Viceroy in Goa in 1667, stated that '...the principal cause of want of the population is the bad conduct of the Portuguese from whose violence the Kaffirs flee to other lands.'

What followed is still to be clarified. But when the German geologist Karl Mauch found the stone walls and buildings in 1871, none of the small number of people living in the area could tell him who had built them. They only knew that quantities of gold had been found there. The natives called the area Zimbabwe — the place of the stones. Writing of his find in a German magazine, Mauch put forward the theory that the area must have been the Biblical land of Ophir — the source of King Solomon's treasure in the tenth century BC. He also observed that the structures were similar to the description of the palace of the Queen of Sheba, so this may have been a replica build in the south.

This remained the accepted theory until 1906, when archaeologist David Randall MacIver examined the site and reported that it had been built by natives and was about six hundred years old. However, the legend persisted for several decades because the settlers in what was then called Rhodesia — mainly of British and South African origin — could or would not accept that black people had built such sophisticated structures.

For this reason the origins of Zimbabwe remained a 'mystery' in government papers and tourist literature. Since regaining control of the country the Africans have named their state Zimbabwe.

Mediterranean Contacts

Greek legends and records refer to Africa outside of Egypt as either Libya — the Libyans being the modern Berbers — or Ethiopia, the land of people with dark faces, and show them to have been in contact with the rest of the known world, living among other peoples on much the same basis as any other foreigners.

Homer not only mentions the Ethiopians but tells us that the Gods of Greece were in the habit of attending feasts in Ethiopia. Eurybiates, the Herald of Agamemnon and Odysseus, is described as Ethiopian and was possibly named after an earlier hero, described as being 'woolly haired and sable skinned'. On the side of the Trojans was Memnon, the nephew of King Priam of Troy. Tradition has it that he was the son of an Ethiopian father. He was the King of Ethiopia and Persia and in depictions on Greek pots is accompanied by black attendants.

Many other images of black people are shown on pots, in sculptures and paintings. Among the images that have come down to us from Greek culture is a small silver coin from the Island of Delphos, which shows the head of a black man on one side. The image is said by scholars to depict either Aesop — the teller of fables, who was thrown to his death from a cliff on Delphos, or Delphenes — the son of Milena, reputed to have set up the Oracle at Delphi.[28]

Images of black people are to be found among the artefacts of the other civilisations of the Mediterranean; the Phoenicians, the Etruscans, the Carthagenians and the Romans. In Carthage on the northern coast of Africa (modern Tunisia), many of the skeletons excavated by archaeologists were of black people. And coins found in the region of Italy once occupied by the armies of Hannibal show elephants on one side and black portraits on the other.[29]

After Rome had defeated Carthage, and established its empire across the Southern Mediterranean, Africa became the oldest and most prized province, and many of Rome's foreign conscripts were drawn from that continent. By the reign of Tiberius, the Third Augustian Legion had become a black corps.[30]

Africa South of the Desert

African development was not confined to the North and East where there was contact with people from other continents. Recent excavations in Nigeria have uncovered many artefacts made from terracotta in the region of Nok, and evidence of iron-working. Tests have revealed that a lively community existed there from about 700 BC to 200 AD. The style of the sculptured objects suggests that they were the forerunners of the elaborate and advanced bronzes of Ife and Benin.

The grassland south of the desert had its own development; from the kingdom of Buganda in the East to Kano and Katsina in the region of Lake Chad. These were trading towns, situated between the desert and the rain forest. They were famous for their leather goods, which were traded as far as Europe, (and incorrectly called Moroccan leather).[31]

On the west coast, the Soninke people established the Kingdom of Ghana, well to the north of the present state that now bears that name. Its power was based on the trade in gold, the flow of which they controlled, as the traders from the north brought in salt from the desert which they traded with the Wangara who were the gold miners.[32]

In the 13th century the Soninke were overthrown by the Mandingo who extended their borders and established the kingdom of Mali. It was during the reign of these rulers that Mali assumed great importance because of its wealth.

In the 15th century the Songhi took power from the Mandingo and held it for over a century. It was lost to an invading force equipped with firearms, sent by the King of Morocco in 1598.

Much can be learned about the position of Africans within their own communities, by referring to certain well-known individuals and incidents. Letters exchanged between King Affonso of the Congo and the King of Portugal from 1514 and 1540, for instance, illustrate the changing pattern of European behaviour on the African continent. Portuguese dealings with Ann Zingha give us some indication of African attitudes to European behaviour and assumptions in their dealings with the people of Angola in the middle of the 17th century. Or a study of the growth of the Zulu nation, under its founder, Shaka,[33] would reveal some of the measures taken by Africans to protect their lives, their land and their way of life from the colonising Europeans.

SECTION TWO

African reactions to slavery and colonisation

II. 1. Ann Zingha

Some African leaders did all that they could to resist the occupation of their land and the acceptance of foreign overlords. Prominent among them was Ann Zingha, who began her resistance to the Portuguese when she was sent as an emissary, by her brother, to arrange a treaty in 1622. A chair was provided for the foreign Viceroy but for her only a cushion on the floor. One of her army of women went down on her hands and knees, and Ann sat on the woman's hips so as to be on the same level as the Viceroy in his chair.

From that position, she refused to pay tribute to the King of Portugal or accept him as overlord.

On becoming Queen after her brother's death, she continued her resistance by every possible means, sometimes taking her army into the bush to continue the fight. She even adopted the Christian faith and appealed to the Pope for independent recognition.

ANN ZINGHA

II. 2. Nanny the Maroon

Those taken across the Atlantic in chains did not always abandon the idea of being free. Whenever possible they would run off into the unexplored regions of the colonies where they formed bands and settlements, living by their wits and skills and occasionally raiding the plantations, taking other slaves away with them. They also encouraged slaves who were brave enough to join them, in spite of the vicious punishments meted out to runaways who were caught.

In Jamaica these runaway slaves, became known as the Maroons. At one stage, they were led by a woman called Nanny who is now considered to have been one of their greatest planners of raids and ambushes, by which means they often defeated the British soldiers sent against them. In the end Britain was forced to sign a treaty which gave the Maroons a free state within the colony.

Nanny is now celebrated as one the first heroes of the Jamaican people.

II. 3. Gustavas Vasa

Some slaves appeared to work with the masters, trying meanwhile to improve the position of their people. They sought changes in the rules governing the behaviour of those in power, changes that would relieve some of the horrors of their conditions. These slaves tried to show their masters that they were just as capable, moral and humane as their European masters, by following the religious practices and behaviour patterns of European society as far as they were permitted.

One such was Olaudah Equanio, or Gustavas Vasa, a former slave who learned to read and was baptised as a Christian. He later bought his freedom from his master, wrote a book about his experiences as a slave and helped in the campaign for the abolition of slavery in England.

II. 4. Toussaint L'Overture

Others combined the two methods: slaves who had been in privileged positions but were not content to remain slaves, tried to lead their people to freedom. Nat Turner led a slave rebellion in America and Toussaint L'Overture led the only successful rebellion of Black Slaves in the New World when he liberated Haiti from the French.

(By permission of the British Library)

II. 5. World War II Poster

However, most black people in the West still live under conditions imposed by the Europeans, and are often involved in the political conflicts of the country in which they live. This World War II poster was used to promote the idea of black people taking part in World War II as members of the British Empire, and black Soldiers from America were later called to defend the beliefs of 'their' country in the wars fought in Korea and Vietnam.

II. 6. (Blacks among the Christians)

This tradition goes back to the 11th-15th centuries, when black people living in the Christian countries fought with the Christians during the Crusades and Holy Wars. This 14th Century book illustration shows the Christian Crusaders taking Jerusulem at the end of the First Crusade in 1099 A.D. Several black knights are depicted.

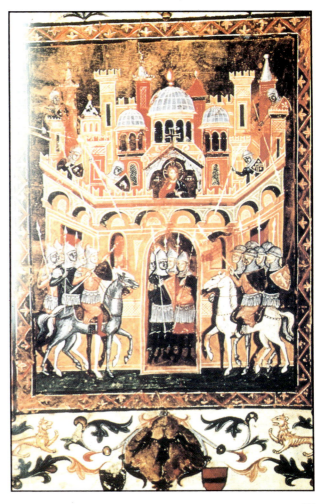

II. 7. Tiepolo — The miracle of St. James

Black people in the Muslim countries also fought for their faith and until the 18th century it was recognised that they were often important leaders during the conflicts.

This painting is by Tiepolo, an Italian painter in the 18th century. It illustrates the story told in Spain, of how St. James the Great emerged from his grave in 939 A.D. during the fighting at Clavijo and helped the Christians, who had been losing the battle, to defeat the Muslims.

The leader of the Muslims is shown as a black man and so are many of his followers. The original occupation of Spain by Muslim armies had been led by a Black man called Tariq ibn Ziyad, and the reinforcement of the Muslims by the Almoravid Sect in 1085 was led by Yusuf ibn Tachfin who was Black or partly so and had Black soldiers as his personal guards.

II. 8. Victory of Heraclius over Chosroes

*The Muslim armies occupied the whole of North Africa and much
of Asia — to the borders of China. When the religious wars began,
the flow of black people from Africa to Europe was cut off. The
number of black people in Europe decreased over the years and
they became associated with the Muslim world. So much so, that
in some European paintings and book illustrations of the 14th and
15th centuries, a black head on a flag was used to indicate
the Muslim forces.*

*This painting by Piero de la Francesca: 'The Victory of Heraclius
over Chosroes' shows two black heads on the banner of the forces
fighting against the Christians. However, the event he is relating
occurred before the founder of the Muslim faith was even born.*

II. 9. The Triumph of Caesar

Until Christian Europe cut itself off from Muslim North Africa, black people had been present in all the large societies and empires around the Mediterranean Sea.

This panel from Mantegna's series 'The Triumph of Caesar' is now at Hampton Court. Painted in the 15th Century, it shows a black soldier in the Roman Armies of Caesar when he invaded Gaul. Another panel shows a black musician.

II. 10. — The Alexander Mosaic

Images of Black soldiers were often drawn on Greek pots and many Greek paintings show black people. In this famous mosaic, the lance held in Alexander's hand is aimed not at the Persian King Darius, but at the black figure falling from a horse, who appears to be on the side of the Greeks.

It is possible that this is a symbolic representation of the killing of the Greek Calvary leader Cleitus, who was dubbed 'Cleitus the Black' by Alexander in a quarrel after both had been drinking.

II. 11. — Memnon and Squire

Earlier Greek works portray black people, in positions of power and authority.

Illustrations from the Legends of the Trojan Wars often show Memnon as black or, where his face cannot be seen as in this image from a pot in the British Museum, in the company of black attendant or squire. He was the nephew of Priam, King of Troy and brought a large army, of both black and white soldiers, to assist his uncle in the defence of the city. He was killed by the Greek hero, Achilles in the battle.

II. 12. — Nubian Soldiers in Egypt

Black people were involved in the events of the Middle East long before the Greeks rose to power. Over two thousand years earlier they contributed to the development of the Nile civilisation of Upper Egypt, Lower Egypt and Nubia.

Nubians in Egypt worked as Officials and Priests. After the two Egypts joined together, the Egyptians became more powerful than their Nubian neighbours, and the Nubians were forced to pay tribute and supply men for the Egyptian armies.

II. 13. — Sphinx

It now appears that many of the early rulers of Egypt were themselves black: many statues of Pharaohs of that period have African features. The best known monument of Egypt — the Sphinx — has the features of an African and is said to be a portrait of King Cheops of the Fourth Dynasty of Egypt. It is now disfigured, as the result of the fighting when Napoleon Bonaparte invaded Egypt early in the 19th century AD.

We have argued in this book for a study of the created artefacts of Africa and its history prior to the West African slave trade. It is important in correcting the false image of black people that exists today.

It is hoped that this second set of images has indicated how black people played an active part in their own liberation from that recent period of slavery, as well as in the early formation of Urban Civilisation as it developed around the Mediterranean and later spread northwards into Europe.

SECTION TWO

African Reactions to Slavery and Colonisation

Teachers' Notes

In his *Guide to African History,* Basil Davidson shows how the relationship of mutual respect that initially existed between the Europeans and the Africans changed to distrust, enmity and hatred.[1]

The Africans were aware at an early stage of the damage being done to their society but were powerless to stop it. This is evident in the letters of King Affonso (Nzinga Mbemba) of the Congo to the king of Portugal in the period 1514 to 1540. The African ruler wrote asking the Portuguese king to stop Portuguese merchants from buying slaves in his kingdom, because the situation had gone beyond his control. The merchants had gone from one chief to another offering to trade goods, alcohol and firearms. The last they would sell only to those who provided them with slaves. They sought out the unscrupulous and those they could ply with drink. Soon others were forced to join in the selling of slaves or else they would have no firearms to defend themselves from those who had. In order to protect themselves, many African chiefs became principal slave traders. Later, the Ashanti Federation of Tribes was formed, to protect the people of the area and to prosper from the trade in slaves.[2]

At that stage few efforts were made to colonise areas of Africa. The only early colonists were the Portuguese, who invaded Mozambique and, later, Angola.[3]

In Angola they met with stern resistance from Ann Zingha (or Nzingha). She was the sister of the King of Angola at the time the Portuguese came. In 1622 she was sent by her brother to negotiate a treaty with the foreigners. She arrived at the appointed place, leading her army of women and found that whereas the Portuguese viceroy had a large chair, there was only a cushion on the floor for her to sit on. One of her followers went down on her hands and knees and Ann sat across her hips, so as to be on the same level as the viceroy in his chair. From that position, she refused to pay tribute to the King of Portugal or to accept him as overlord.[4]

Ann accepted the Christian faith but insisted on the independence of her country. On the death of her brother, she became Queen. The Portuguese sent an army against her. In defeat she was offered the retention of her position on condition that she agreed to pay tribute. She refused, fled into the bush with her army, renounced Christianity and continued the fight from the bush for eighteen years. She later returned to the faith, but whether as the result of the work of missionaries or whether as a means of continuing her struggle, no-one knew.

She was restored to her throne, but could not be persuaded to accept the Portuguese as overlords. She appealed to the Pope for recognition of her independent position and asked him to send missionaries to her country. In 1663 she died at the age of eighty-one.

During the years of her leadership, Nzingha established a reputation as fierce in battle but generous to her defeated enemies. So much so, that even European writers who vilified her as a virago addicted to the use of arms, were forced to admit that she never killed an enemy soldier who had surrendered, and that those under her command honoured her instructions.

Slave Rebellions in the New World

In the Americas, the Africans did all they could to avoid remaining slaves. One strategy was to escape into the forests and unoccupied regions of the new colonies and form bands to resist the slave hunters and soldiers sent to recapture them. Two such groups were the Djuka of Surinam and the Maroons of Jamaica.

The Djuka fought against the Dutch and established a free colony in Surinam 100 years before slavery was abolished in that colony.[5]

In Jamaica, helped by the fighting between the Spanish and the British, large numbers of slaves escaped into the hills. There they established fortified positions, resisted recapture and raided the plantations, sometimes taking away slaves to increase their numbers. One of their leaders, Nanny, proved to be a brilliant tactician, planning raids and ambushes of the soldiers sent against them. At another period, their leader Cudjoe negotiated a treaty with the British, establishing a free colony known as the Maroon State within Jamaica in 1739.[6] The only other group to succeed in doing this were slaves in Brazil, who escaped into the forest and established a republic called Palmeres.

The Maroon colony began in the seventeenth century and there were many changes of fortune during the long Maroon wars. As in all such situations, there were individuals willing to betray the cause of their people for their own personal gain. One such was Juan de Bolas, a leader of one of the Maroon bands. He surrendered to the British in return for his own freedom and immunity, and in 1657 he was made Colonel of a regiment of black soldiers and sent out to help in the capture of his former comrades, which he did with limited success.

To discourage black slaves from running away, harsh punishments were introduced by law. The slave colonies of the Caribbean and the Americas became one vast concentration camp for Africans. In 1733, for example, there was a revolt in St Johns, because of laws passed the previous year, decreeing the following punishments:

> For leading others to run away: pinched three times with a hot iron followed by hanging. For following others in a run away: a leg cut off or, if pardoned by the master, ears cut off and 150 lashes applied.
>
> Failing to report a runaway or the planning of an escape: burned on the forehead and 100 lashes.
>
> Absence for eight days: 150 lashes.
>
> Absence for twelve weeks: loss of a leg.
>
> Absence for six months: death.
>
> For lifting a hand to strike a white person or threatening violence: pinched with hot irons and hanged.[7]

Those who were too frightened to resist were regarded as 'servile and meek', even 'cowardly'. The black man's character could thus be defined by whites as 'violent' or 'cringing', as it suited them.

In spite of and, at times, because of such treatment, slave revolts were a regular feature of colonial life in the Americas. There were revolts in British

Guyana, in many of the small islands and in the American colonies, later the United States: where the best known was led by an educated slave called Nat Turner. However, the only completely successful rebellion was led by Toussaint L'Overture, who liberated Haiti from the French.[8]

Black Resistance to Slavery in England

The runaway slave in England was an element in the changing situation at the end of the eighteenth century but, as in other ways, there was a great difference in how they were treated. Punishments for running away in England were never as severe as in the colonies.

In 1772, Lord Mansfield ruled that slaves arriving in England should be considered free men, supporting a judgement made in 1749 by Chief Justice Holt. The Mansfield judgement was given in the case of James Somerset, whose case was supported by members of the Abolitionist Movement.

Granville Sharp had become an active member of the Abolitionist Movement after he had discovered a slave called Jonathan Strong who had been badly beaten and thrown out by his master. Such was Strong's condition that he had to remain at St Bartholomew's hospital for three months.

Two years later, his former owner, David Lisle, saw the recovered man on the street. Lisle plotted his recapture, then sold him to a Jamaican planter. Strong was put in prison until the ship which was to take him away was ready to sail. He managed to get a message to Sharp, who visited him in prison and obtained his release. Lisle took Sharp to court but ultimately, Strong was set free.[9]

Other slaves sought their freedom by conforming to the system and attempting to prove to their masters, that they were morally and intellectually worthy human beings. Among these were Francis Barber, the servant of Dr. Johnson. Johnson encouraged and paid for Barber's education and he eventually became a school teacher.

Ignatius Sancho was another. Of African heritage, he had taught himself to read and write and, under the patronage of the Duke of Montague, he became popular in the literary and artistic circles of his time and his writings widely read. He was a friend of Dr. Johnson, Lawrence Sterne, sculptor Joseph Noekens, and he had his portrait painted by Gainsborough in 1768.

Perhaps the most famous was Olaudah Equiano, also known as Gustavas Vasa/Vassa. In 1743 as a child of ten, Equiano was taken from Biafra and became slave to a Captain Phillips, with whom he sailed the Mediterranean, the Atlantic and the Caribbean. During a spell ashore, he was put with a family in Greenwich, where he learned to read and write, and was baptised as a Christian. His master was suspicious of this baptism fearing that Equiano was following the custom among the Muslims in Africa, still prevalent among the slaves, where baptism as a Christian was seen as a prelude to obtaining their freedom. Suspecting that Equiano was planning to run away, he sold him to an American planter.

Eventually Equiano bought his freedom from his American master and returned to London, where he worked as a hairdresser for twenty years. In 1773 he took part in the Phipps expedition to the Arctic, and on his return, began to work as an abolitionist and black activist. In 1783 he sought the support of Grenville Sharpe in his campaign to have the deaths of 132 Africans thrown overboard from the slave-ship Zong treated as a mass murder. The two men continued to be a significant combined force in the abolitionist struggle.

When an expedition was planned to take black settlers to Sierra Leone, Equiano was appointed as Commissary. But he was dismissed from this post following his exposure of Joseph Iwin, Government Agent, who had been abusing the scheme for his own profit. Equiano was later vindicated.

In 1789 he published his experiences as a slave and as a free black living in London: *Interesting Narrative of the Life of Olaudah Equiano, or Gustavas Vassa, The African*. It was the first time that a black writer had or a wide set out public. It attracted a great deal of comment and aroused public opinion in support of the abolitionist cause.

Ottobah Cugano followed in the footsteps of Equiano and, probably in collaboration with him, published *Thoughts and Sentiments on the Evil and Wicked Traffic of Slavery and the Commerce of the Human Species* in 1788, in which he systematically demolished the arguments in favour of slavery.

The British Worker and the Black Slave

The presence of slaves in England and the struggle for their freedom prompted comparisons with the condition of the working class during the Industrial Revolution, particularly after the Closure Act forced many subsistence farmers into the towns and factories. There were cases of whole families being forced to work up to seventeen hours a day. Workers in mines and on farms suffered similar conditions, and invited comparison with the lot of slaves on Caribbean plantations. The recruitment of sailors by Press Gangs, the obtaining of soldiers by trickery and the punishment administered: keel-hauling and flogging sailors and flogging soldiers, were also similar to the way slaves were captured and treated. Being a soldier was virtually a life sentence. Such was the social standing of the British soldier in the 18th century that one table of preferences was: 'a messmate before a shipmate, a shipmate before a stranger, a stranger before a dog and a dog before a soldier'. ('The Making of the British' *Observer Magazine* 3/8/1975). As late as the Battle of Waterloo, Wellington is said to have described his foot-soldiers as 'the scum of the Earth.'

Campaigns for better conditions for British workers — for a fourteen-hour and, later, a ten-hour day — ran concurrently with the campaign for abolition of slavery. In 1818 the Factory Act banned the employment of children under nine years of age in some areas of factory production, but it was not until 1833 — the same year as the abolition of slavery — that children in the textile industry (though not those in the silk mills) were accorded the same rights as other children.[10]

After 1833 the struggle of the British working class continued. Groups from the north of England joined with the Birmingham Political Union and the London Working Men's Association to oppose the Poor Law in the years 1836 to 1848. They produced a People's Charter and the resulting movement became known as the Chartist Movement. The Charter demanded: male adult suffrage; secret ballots; equal electoral districts; no property qualification and a salary for Members of Parliament; annual elections for Parliament.[11]

There were fears that the movement would result in revolution, as in France, and it was suppressed. But the demands continued in the face of Government opposition. In our time most of the demands have been met by legislation, under pressure from Trade Unions.

'Free' Blacks Under White Domination

The abolitionists argued that the humanity of slaves should be respected, symbolised by their emblem of a kneeling slave and the words *Am I Not a Man and a Brother?* Those wishing to maintain slavery tried to prove that black people were innately inferior, and argued that their own positions of power and wealth were justified on moral, social, intellectual and religious grounds.

When slavery was abolished little provision was made for 'free' blacks. They were simply told that they were free and given no means of providing for themselves. In the colonies, their condition amounted to a continuation of slavery. The newly freed slaves had no means of having their grievances taken into account, nor were their customs and religious practices treated with respect.

The only method left to the powerless for getting their grievances aired was by revolt. When they did so, the Europeans assumed the role of the wronged party who had simply been caring for those who could not look after themselves. Indeed, it was 'the white man's burden' to look after lesser breeds; these uprisings were just another example of the innate savagery, evil intent and ingratitude of the blacks.

This thinking was applied to the Indian uprising in 1857, supported by Nana Sahib and the Rhani of Jhansi, and to the Morant Bay rebellion in Jamaica in 1865, led by George Bogle and supported by George William Gordon. Both followed abolition and both were used by those in authority to 'prove' to European people that the black people were cruel, vengeful and morally inferior to themselves; although in both cases, the British Army had exacted a ten-fold revenge.

By the start of this century, large areas of the world were under British domination and known as the British Empire. The colonies were so extensive and so scattered that 'the sun', it was said 'never set on the British Empire'. In the first World War, the people of the occupied territories were marshalled to the aid of their colonial masters. Britain continued its practice of getting former slaves to fight on their side as soldiers. Black soldiers, some from the West Indies, had fought for the British in the Wars of American Independence.[12]

The *Grenada Handbook and Directory* 1946 records the involvement of the British West Indies Regiment in 1914-1918. The first contingent of volunteers reached England in autumn, 1915 and that November was formally recognised as the British West Indies Regiment. It eventually comprised of 15,204 men, eleven battalions. They served in France, East Africa, Mesopotamia, Egypt and the Jordan Valley. At first they were mainly employed on ammunition duties, loading and unloading ammunition at roads and railheads, and humping shells for the heavy guns. They were praised by Lord Haig in a dispatch from France for the part they played 'carrying ammunition up to the batteries. This work has been very arduous and has been carried out almost continuously under Shell-fire'. Later they were allowed to take their place in the firing line and acquitted themselves with honour, particularly in the Jordan Valley. At the end of the War, 185 were listed as killed in action, 1,071 died of illnesses, 697 were wounded, 81 were awarded medals and 49 were mentioned in dispatches.

During the second World War many black people enlisted in the British Air Force and various Army regiments. In the Caribbean, thousands served in the Home Guard. Camps were set up in many islands to guard against possible attack from the enemy and to deter the setting up of base camps. The whole population of the area contributed to the British war effort, whether in money, as contributed to the Air Force by the Jamaican Government or in scrap-iron for munitions factories gathered by school children.

At the end of World War I, the soldiers returned to the colonies as willing citizens of a colonial Empire. But at the end of World War II, there was discontent over returning to the poor conditions in the colonies. The first group to take action were a party of former airmen and soldiers who returned to an intolerable social, economic and political situation in Jamaica. They chartered a ship — the *Empire Windrush* —and returned to England to seek employment, causing consternation. Questions were raised about the implication of this action in the Houses of Parliament, and in the press. Others followed, later joined by relatives and friends. So began the migration of people from the British Caribbean to England in the 1950s and 60s.[13]

The impact of the Wars was even greater in Africa, precipitating the decolonisation of Africa, as well as change in African perceptions of Europeans. The ways that the consequences of the war affected Africa are worthy of study (see reading list on p.60).

Crowder (1984) tells of two and a half million Africans involved as troops and carriers in the first World War and about a million sent to Europe and the Far East in the second. Millions of Africans were involved, in activities ranging from commercial and clerical to road-building and food supply.

In World War I, it was claimed that the Africans were volunteers but this was not so. In some French colonies such as the Gold Coast, there was conscription to a degree described as 'a full-scale manhunt'. In the British colony of Northern Rhodesia (now Zambia), one third of the adult male population was recruited for military labour. Instructions were given to the Regent of Bakwena to 'compile their list of persons who have not yet responded to the call for recruits'. According to these instructions,'Only those presenting themselves as willing' were to be sent to training camps, while:

> Those who were unwilling should be placed on some form of tribal work so that should they refuse to carry out this work a legitimate charge can be made against them in the Native Courts.

Because of these methods of conscription and recruitment, young men mutilated themselves or they fled to the bush or neighbouring territories. So remorseless was the pursuit of manpower that Jide Osuntokun (1978) has termed it 'the new slave trade'.

World War II had an even greater impact in terms of initiating radical social, economic and political changes. The soldiers, particularly those who served in Europe and the Far East, were not only subjected to the propaganda that they were fighting for the preservation of freedom and democracy but they were also made aware of their own lack of political freedom and democracy; and some witnessed, in India, fellow colonials protesting against Britain's restrictions on their freedom. With almost a million men returning to Africa with broadened views of the world and higher expectations for themselves and their country, the stage was set for reform. Not surprisingly, the first incident to open the gates of freedom, the riots of Accra in 1948, were triggered by ex-servicemen demonstrating against their living conditions. That incident ultimately led to the independence of Ghana, and gradually of the rest of Africa.

Before the second World War, Africans had generally viewed Europeans as a clan with special skills and knowledge who, by virtue of the colour of their skin, were sacrosanct, but the events of the war changed that. Crowder (1984) ends his account with this quote from *Stepping Stones,* the memoirs of Sylvia Leith-Ross, who spent much of her life in Nigeria:

> The mass of the people still thought of the white race as one, united by colour, education, religion. All these white men were rich, and had come into the world with ready-made knowledge and skills. Therefore, for the time being, they dominated the African...

> Every time we indicted Germany, we indicted ourselves as well. Except for the travelled or highly educated few, Europeans had been a mass conception for so long that whatever cruelty or treachery or injustice we attributed to our enemies was seen as a possible attribute of ourselves.

> Further, outside and apart from our own propaganda directed against a section of fellow-Europeans, another and even more radical change, noted by few, was taking place in the black-white attitude of the masses... Perhaps for the first time, except in individual cases, an element of contempt had crept into their minds: these 'Civilised' white men could nevertheless kill each other in great numbers, their rich towns could be

destroyed, their expensive homes burnt down, they could be tortured and starved, they could cringe and beg for help and for money. And, curious sidelight emerging from conversations with observant Africans who had been in contract with our troops or sailors, for the first time in their lives these Africans had met a number of Europeans *less educated than themselves*... They were careful to show no disdain, only sheer amazement that they should have been mistaken. You could not help feeling that this discovery was perhaps the final insidious blow which shattered the crumbling edifice of white superiority.

The Wars also contributed to changes for black people in the United States. When World War I began, the laws of segregation introduced during the period of reconstruction following the American Civil War were still in force. African-Americans were forced to live in restricted areas and had little control over their own lives. They were barred from any meaningful political activity and terrorised by white extremist organisations such as the Klu Klux Klan. In his book *Roots*, Alex Haley tells of black soldiers returning to the United States after the war, being gunned down in the streets by members of the Klan, who saw them as a potential threat to the existing order. There were cases of black people taken from their homes and lynched, simply because Jack Johnson had become the first black man to win the heavyweight boxing championship.

After the second World War, pressures from black organisations on the Law Courts led to the desegregation of schools in some areas of the Southern States. With increased awareness, blacks in Alabama refused to ride on segregated buses. The Reverend Martin Luther King was elected to organise the operation of the strike and its ultimate success propelled him to the forefront of the struggle for desegregation and the demands for racial equality.

The war in Korea involved great numbers of young black men in military activity but, ultimately it was the war in Vietnam that brought the matter of Civil Rights to a head. As American casualties mounted, it became obvious that a disproportionate number of black men were being sent to the battle zone and this was reflected in the casualties. The cry went up that black Americans were dying for a country in which their civil rights were not respected. Black people in America were living under civil conditions similar to those of colonial people. Now the newly independent nations of Africa served as models for black independence within the United States.

Actions both civil and legal were taken. There were sit-ins to demand the desegregation of lunch counters, demands for voting rights and marches and demonstrations in support of various actions. While the traditional organisations demanded civil rights, breakaway groups pressed still further. There were demands for Black power: the Black Panthers — veterans of Vietnam — openly advocated armed struggle, and the Black Muslims made demands for the partitioning of the United States, to allow black people an area in which they could be independent. For several years the controversies rocked America and riots flared in several of its cities. In this way, many of the liberties now taken for granted by the young were obtained.

Black resistance to slavery in the United States

Slavery continued in the United States for nearly three decades after it was abolished in Britain and its Colonies. It was only brought to its end by a bloody Civil War which began in 1861.

As in all the slave colonies in the New World, the slaves had never accepted their conditions as permanent and there had been several rebellions, the best documented being that led by Nat Turner. There were also individual acts of rebellion and large numbers of slaves ran away. Some of the runaways were assisted by members of European religious groups opposed to slavery, such as Quakers (the Society of Friends). Others joined the indigenous Indian people where circumstances permitted — to this day there are many African-Americans with Indian strains in their ancestry — while still others bought their freedom, where allowed. So there were 'free' blacks in America before it ceased to be a British Colony. Indeed it is said that one of the first persons to die for the freedom of the United States was a runaway slave called Crispus Attucks. Born a slave in Massachusetts in 1723, he had run away from his master and worked as a sailor on ships out of Boston. He became an active member of a group called the Sons of Liberty and, with two others, was shot by a British soldier on Dock Square, in one of the incidents which led to the famous Boston Tea Party and, ultimately, to the wars of Independence.[14]

A century later, another runaway slave was to make his mark in Massachusetts when he addressed the Anti-slavery Society of that city in 1841. He was Frederick Douglas, the son of a white man and a black part-Indian slave woman. He made such an impression that he was asked to become an agent of the society and later became a leader in the movement against slavery. In 1845 he published

The Narrative of the life of Frederick Douglas. To avoid capture, he travelled to Britain, where he spent two years campaigning against slavery in the United States. On his return he started a newspaper, the *North Star,* which functioned for seventeen years.

When the civil war began, Douglas helped to organise two regiments of black soldiers and encouraged black people to take up arms with the Union Army. By the end of the war he held several government posts, the last being as American Minister to Haiti.[15]

A notable contemporary of Frederick Douglas was Harriet Tubman. She too had escaped to freedom in the North, travelling by night, hiding by day, until she reached Philadelphia where she found work as a cook. There she heard of a secret organisation known as the Underground Railway which helped people to escape, as she had done. She volunteered for service with the group, knowing that the work was dangerous. Under the Fugitive Slave Act of 1850, escaped slaves found anywhere in the United States had to be returned to their owners. This meant that to find safety they had to be taken to Canada.[16]

In spite of her poor health, Tubman is credited with nineteen excursions into the South, so leading over three hundred slaves to freedom, including her own parents. Such was her fame that she earned the name of Moses among the slaves. A reward of forty thousand dollars was offered for her capture by the authorities of the Southern States.

During the Civil War, Harriet Tubman worked as a cook, a nurse and then as a spy for the Union Army, gathering information behind the Confederate lines and encouraging slaves to join the Union Forces. After the war she lived in Auburn, New York where she founded a home for old black people.

Another active campaigner of the time was the Reverend Hiram Revels, pastor of a Methodist Church in Baltimore, Maryland and principal of a school for black children in the City. During the Civil War he left his pulpit to recruit soldiers to form the first black regiment from Maryland. He also helped to recruit for other regiments of the Union Army and served as a regiment chaplain.[17]

After the war, Revels became minister of the Methodist Episcopal Church in Natchez, Mississippi, where he established himself as an able leader within the community. He was invited to enter politics and, after some consideration, he ran for the post of alderman and was elected in 1868. He was later elected to the Mississippi State Senate and then as Senator for the State of Mississippi, so becoming the first black person to sit in the Senate of the United States. Some years later he was followed by Blanche K Bruce, a former fugitive slave who had established a school for black pupils in Hannibal, Missouri, and had served ably in several local offices.

The achievements of these activist were later to be negated by concessions made to the Southern States in the interest of re-unification. They were allowed to introduce 'Jim Crow' State Laws which effectively barred black people from positions of power and segregated them from the white community. The effect of this was further intensified by the tacit acceptance — or even active support — given to white terror organisations, particularly the Klu Klux Klan, by large sections of the community, politicians and law enforcement officers. Black leaders were often killed and no attempt made to bring their killers to justice. Where the killers were known, they were often released by juries who were not prepared to convict them. Blacks who challenged the system or offended in any way were quite likely to be lynched by mobs or taken away by hooded men at night to be found dead the next day.

Black organisations such as the Urban League and the National Association for the Advancement of Coloured People did what they could for the protection of black people and did much to change the system by constitutional means. Major changes, however, took place in the wake of the Second World War. The National Guard had to be called out to supervise the de-segregation of schools at Little Rock, Arkansas, and it took the leadership of the Reverend Martin Luther King to achieve desegregation of buses and a campaign to get lunch counters desegregated. The campaigns created turmoil throughout the United States in the 1950s and 1960s and many new leaders emerged. Some, like Hughie Norton and Eldridge Cleaver, faded into oblivion. The influence of others, such as Elija Mohamed, leader of the Black Muslims, Malcolm X, and Stockley Carmichael (now know as Kwame Turve) is still with us.

The old tradition

The fact that black people living in areas of the world dominated by Europeans, fight for or with their European rulers, is not a new or strange occurrence. There is a long history of conquered people taking part in conflicts, on the side of their conquerors.

The tradition of black people fighting as allies of whites is an old one in Western Society. Sometimes this was because they had established a method of co-existence with their conquerors. At other times the alliances were the result of a common religious or political belief. During the Crusades there had been black people among the Christians and also among the Muslims: we see evidence of this in the book illustrations and works of art which have come down to us from that period of soon afterwards.[18]

One can look back to the Roman Imperial era when political action by the state created disagreements among the Early Christians. Roman North Africa was one of the main strongholds of Christianity at the time when the Edict of Decius was issued in 250 AD, compelling all citizens to perform a sacrifice to the pagan Gods in the presence of commissioners appointed by the state. The commissioners then issued a 'Certificate of Loyalty'. The Edict was aimed at the Christians and those who refused to sacrifice to the gods were classified as 'subversives' and subject to punishment. Generally this meant imprisonment, but for priests and bishops the punishment was often death in the arena.[19]

Many Christians became aposate, while others obtained certificates by dishonest means such as bribery. Those obtaining certificates by such means came to be known as the 'libella tici'. Anxious to maintain its membership, many leaders of the Church, including St Cyprian, were prepared to accept them still as Christians and even to allow them to hold office. Others were against such forgiveness, as the same allowances were not made for the poor who had 'lapsed' as Christians in order to save their lives. Those who had been imprisoned or tortured came to be treated as heroes and regarded as the rightful leaders of the Faith, much to the annoyance and amazement of the bishops and deacons who had managed to avoid imprisonment. The result was that many accusations and cross-accusations were made.

The rift deepened when the Roman authorities strove to confiscate the written scriptures and items used in ceremonies, such as candlesticks. Attempts were made to obtain confessions and information from those captured in raids. Those who gave information to save themselves were called traitors, and when they were treated in the same manner as the 'libella tici', open opposition broke out within the Church, led by Donatus, a Bishop of Carthage.

After several decades of dispute, the quarrel was taken to the Synod of Arles in 314 AD and judgement went against the Donatists. An appeal to the Synod of Milan two years later met with the same result. By then Constantine had issued his Edict of Milan and the Christians were no longer persecuted but the Synod ruled that the Donatists were heretics and their property and civil rights were taken away. However, they continued to function in North Africa and in 411 AD a conference at Carthage again branded them as heretics and denied them right of assembly. Thus was the Christian Church of Africa separated from the Churches of Europe, then mainly in Italy and France.

The decision made by Diocletian to divide the Empire into Eastern and Western sections helped to separate European Christianity from that of the East (Asia).

After his death, Constantine re-united the Empire by conquering Macentius. It was before that encounter that Constantine is said to have had a vision of a cross bearing the words *In hoc signo vinces* — 'By this sign thou shall conquer'. After his victory he gave his support to the Christians and made Christianity the official religion of the state. In 330 AD he moved his capital to Constantinople. The new state religion was serviced under the leadership of the Bishops of Rome and of Constantinople, thus dividing the Church into Eastern and Western Churches.

After the sacking of Rome in 410 AD, the Church of Constantinople held sway and in time came to be known as Byzantium. Europe became a collection of fragmentated states, controlled by Franks, Goths and Normans during what has come to be known as the 'Dark Ages'. But many had been converted to the Christian faith and contact with what remained of Roman culture and social organisation became the model for their society.

A third factor came into play: the rise of Islam. By the end of the seventh century, the followers of Mohamed had spread out of Arabia and had taken over Persia, parts of Egypt and most of North Africa. In 711 they crossed into Spain and nine years later were on the borders of France. There they were halted by an army of Franks under the leadership of Charles Martel.[20] They withdrew into Spain where they remained in control until the start of the thirteenth century, when all the Moors, except those in the province of Granada, were driven from Spain.

In 768 Charlemagne — the grandson of Charles Martel — became King of the Franks and immediately set about expanding his territory, conquering the Lombards in Italy, the Saxons to the north and the Baravians in the East. He attacked the Moors in Spain several times, the most notable ending in disaster at Roncesvalles in 778. Roland, Margrave of Brittany is said to have died a hero's death at that battle. The romantic version of his heroism was told in the *Chanson de Roland* and his exploits became a model and source of inspiration for the European Knights of the Crusades.[21]

In 800 AD, Charlemagne was crowned as Carolus Augustus, Emperor of the Romans, by Pope Leo III. This was the final repudiation of the claims of suzerainty by the rulers and the Pope of the East (Byzantium). Charlemagne became the Emperor of the Holy Roman Empire and the rulers of the Western European Kingdoms accepted the religious leadership of the Popes of Rome. The European Church, already separated from the church of North Africa, now became separated from Christianity in the East. This was further underlined by the sacking of Byzantium by the European Knights of the Fourth Crusade.

The First Crusade had ostensibly been launched against the Seliuk Turks, because they had placed restrictions on Christian missionaries to Jerusalem after they overran the area in 1071. In time, the desire to 'free' Jerusalem was linked to the reconquest of Spain from the Moors. The Pope had decreed that all sins committed or likely to be committed would be forgiven to those who took arms in the cause of Christ, and rulers offered to share the booty of goods taken from the conquered heathens. In time, conquest led to power and all who were not Christians became potential victims of Christian conquest. In 1208-13, the Albigensians were attacked and this was followed by an invasion of the Baltic States by the Teutonic Knights.[22]

While the Crusades involved several European rulers working together and helped to cement the idea of a united Christendom, they did not preclude the rulers from fighting among themselves. The Third Crusade was led by Richard I of England and Phillip II of France. On his way back to England, Richard was kidnapped and held for ransom by Henry IV of Germany. On being set free, Richard remained in England for only a few months before setting off for war against his former ally, Phillip of France.

Richard is known as the Lion Heart because of his bravery in battle but his devotion to the Crusading cause was financed by reckless and ruthless means. One way of raising money was heavily to tax the Jewish communities who had become rich and powerful as money-lenders and merchant bankers. Many of the wealthier Jews were dispossessed of their property. Taking their lead from the King, many of his followers descended on the Jewish quarters of London and York and plundered their homes, so earning Richard a reputation as a persecutor of the Jews.

As the conflict progressed the Mediterranean became a divider separating Christian Europe from Moslem North Africa, and as their numbers among the Europeans decreased, the black people became increasingly identified with the Moslem world. Added to the established belief that the Prophet Mohamed was black, black people became identified with the 'enemy'. We can see this in European paintings of the early Renaissance.

In Giotto's series of the life of Christ, the only black is the figure striking at Christ in the panel depicting 'The Mocking'. Black people are shown among those executing St George, in a painting by Mantegena. Another work on the same subject by Altichicro, in the Oratory of St George in Padua, shows a black head emblem on the armour of the chief presiding officer, and on a shield held by one of the soldiers. The theme of identifying blacks with the forces ranged against Christianity is taken further in two works by Pierro de la Francesca. One is the much damaged 'Victory of Constantine over Maxentius', in which there is just enough of the banner left to show that a black head was used as the emblem which identified the forces of Maxentius. In the other, 'The Victory of Heraclius over Chosoroes' from the series of the Legend of the True Cross, shows two black heads on the banner of the forces of Chosoroes, the heathen ruler from the East who had taken the cross from its rightful place.

Blacks among the Romans and Greeks

From the Christian point of view, and from a perspective which turns a blind eye to the part they played in the early establishment of the faith, black people are also identified as followers of those religions with which the early Christians were in conflict. The most important of these was the worship of Isis. This religion, which has its origins in the early dawn of Egyptian society, had been taken up by many Romans after their occupation of Egypt, and scenes depicting aspects of its ceremonies were found painted on the walls of Pompeii and the surrounding area, which for several centuries were covered by the volcanic ash from the eruption of Mount Vesuvius in 79 AD. The paintings show the active presence of black priests officiating in the ceremonies. In other parts of the Empire, evidence of the religious practice have also been found, including at a Temple unearthed in the City of London.

After the Roman occupation of North Africa, many black people joined the Roman armies. By the reign of Tiberius, the Third Augustian Legion had become a black corps, and Roman records have established that black soldiers were sent to other parts of the Empire.[23] Records show that some were stationed along Hadrian's Wall, on the border between England and Scotland. The city of York was first set up as a Roman garrison, under the command of an African general Petillius Cerealis. The Roman Emperor Septimus Serverus, a Libyan by birth, spent time there as General, and returned in his last years, dying in 211 AD.

In their rise to power, the Romans fought many battles with the Carthagenians, recorded in Roman history as the Punic Wars, Punii being the Roman name for the Carthagenians. Large numbers of black soldiers fought among the Carthagenians, and many of the records and objects at the time record their presence. Small statues of elephants — closely associated with the best-known Carthagenian leader, Hannibal — show the animals being handled by black men, and the coins of the Carthagenians found in the region of Northern Italy occupied by the armies of Hannibal for twelve years, depict elephants on one side and a black portrait on the other.[24] It is now believed that Hannibal himself was a black African.

The Carthagenians also fought several battles against the Greeks and were one of the major powers in the Mediterranean for several centuries before their conflicts with the Romans. Their encounters with the Greeks have come down to us through Greek records so, naturally, the Carthagenians are cast in an unfavourable light. From these records it is known that large numbers of black soldiers were captured and enslaved when the Carthagenians landed an army on Sicily in 480 BC,[25] and again when the Carthagenian General, Himilco abandoned his army at Syracuse in 396 BC.

Blacks are also on record as on the side of the Greeks. Probably the most noteworthy was Cleitus, sometimes referred to as Cleitus the Black, or Black Cleitus. He was King of Bactia and commander of the Greek calvary under Phillip of Macedon, father of Alexander the Great, and he maintained that position under Alexander, to whom he was a close companion. Various histories of Alexander tell of their close relationship, and how Cleitus had saved Alexander's life at least once by getting the better of a Persian called Spithradates, who was about to strike Alexander a fatal blow.[26] However, after the conquest of the Persians, when both men were in a state of intoxication, Alexander grabbed a spear from one of the guards and killed Cleitus during a fit of rage.

In fact, and fiction, black soldiers were recorded taking part in Greek conflicts, both as friend and foe, long before Alexander's birth. Homer writes of black soldiers fighting for the Greeks and the Trojans.

Memnon, King of Ethiopia and Persia headed an army of which half the soldiers were black. His mission was to assist King Priam of Troy, his uncle. He was traditionally the son of a black father and a white mother, and is often depicted as black, or in the company of black attendants.

On the side of the Greeks, there was Eurybiates, the black herald of Theseus and Agamemnon, probably named after an earlier hero whose exploits were unrecorded, but to whom reference is made by Homer, describing him as 'woolly haired' and 'sable-skinned'.

In one tradition of the Greek legends, the hero Hercules is regarded as a person of mixed race and the God Zeus as Ethiopian. In one of his exploits, Hercules visited Egypt where it was the custom of the King Burisis to treat visitors to a feast before sacrificing them to his god. When Hercules realised what was to be his fate, he turned on his captors and killed the King on his own altar.

On many Greek pots Burisis is shown as black. This was possibly due to the fact the the Nubians had conquered Egypt in the eighth century BC, establishing the 25th Dynasty which lasted for about seventy years. It was from these black rulers that the Assyirians took control of Egypt, to be overcome in turn by the Persians.

The Nubians of the 25th Dynasty were not the only black rulers of Egypt, nor even the first. The statues of the 18th Dynasty show the Pharaohs of that period to be black people. The Greek historian, Herodotus, was told that of the four hundred rulers of Egypt, to his time, eighteen had been Ethiopians (black people). The statues of the earliest known Dynasties show the rulers as having African features: among these are Djoser of the 3rd Dynasty and Cheops (said to be the model for the face of the Great Sphinx) from the 4th Dynasty.

Egyptian records tell of battles between themselves and the Nubians from the earliest times but they also tell of Nubian soldiers, tax-gatherers, priests and officials of every king in Egypt.[27] Many historians now believe that Upper Egypt was a Black kingdom before the joining of the two kingdoms when Upper Egypt conquered Lower Egypt. The ruler, Narmer, was the first of the Pharaohs to use the title 'The Ruler with Two Crowns' and most of the Pharaohs to the period of the Hyksos invasion are believed to have been Africans.

According to this school of thought, Egyptian society was the result of tribes gathering along the river Nile, as the climate of the region changed and the once pastoral area dried out into the desert which now stretches across North Africa, Arabia and the Near East. Rock paintings from the area surrounding the Nile and across the Tassili Mountains as far as Tunisia, show that the region was once occupied by a black skinned people who lived by herding cattle. The Nile societies were first grouped into three divisions, Nubia, Upper Egypt and Lower Egypt.

Nubia and Upper Egypt were black kingdoms, while Lower Egypt included many of the light-skinned Berber tribes, and was open to migrants from other countries in and around the Mediterranean as well as the Semitic tribes of the Eastern desert. Some idea of the migrations which took place can be gained by studying the story of Jacob, and the subsequent gathering of the Jews in Egypt, from where they were, eventually, led to freedom from their slave status by Moses.

A short study of the formative and early periods of Egyptian civilisation shows that from the earliest urban civilisation from which Western Culture traces its roots, black people have been present and active within the communities.

Recommended reading

UNESCO *General History of Africa* Vol.VIII Heinemann.

The Cambridge History of Africa Vol.VIII Cambridge University Press.

Imperialism at Bay: The United States and the Decolonisation of British Empire, by William Roger Louis: Oxford University Press, 1977.

The *Journal of African History* Vol IXIX No.1 1978; Jide Osuntokun.

For a concise introduction, *The Impact of Two World Wars on Africa,* by Michael Crowder.

History Today Vol.34 January 1984 is highly recommended (see Bibliography).

SECTION THREE

Religion and the role of Black people

Section II focused on the involvement of black people in military activity throughout history and on images of leaders of resistance groups. African people have also been active in the development of ideas and were at the source of many of the established religions.

The picture collection in Section III illustrates ways that black expertise took other forms beside military activity. Ideas had to be formulated for the political and economic organisation of black people for independence in harmony with European society. It also shows that before the European domination of Africa, African people had helped to formulate many religions and had been active in the fields of philosophy and medicine.

III. I. Aretha Franklyn

Religious observance often includes music and some forms of worship include dances. Black people living in the West have maintained this tradition and its effects have overflowed into popular music.

Aretha Franklyn, a popular singer since the 1960s, has been called the 'Queen of Soul' and has also made hit records of 'Gospel' music. The daughter of a Baptist preacher, she began her career in the choir of the church. The choirs of black churches in the United States can be regarded as a training ground for popular music, as shown by the number of famous singers who began singing in church choirs.

III. 2. Bob Marley

Music and religion have also been combined in the career of Bob Marley, the first singer from the so-called 'Third World' to achieve international fame. Through his influence, Reggae music of Jamaica became popular around the world. The earliest Reggae performers, including Bob Marley himself, were followers and practioners of the Rastafarian religion.

III. 3. Baptism in a river

Religion plays a large part in the life of black people all over the world. Where it takes the form of Christian belief, it is sometimes depicted as exotic in its black expression and adaptation of the faith, embodying the African traditions of music and dance in the celebration of its practice.

III. 4. Black church goers (with tambourines etc.)

This attitude has been fostered by the established churches, which have used the principle of portraying black people as exotic or primitive in their missionary work in Africa and other parts of the world.

III. 5. Black people, white priest

In this way black people are portrayed as being converted from a heathen paganism by the white missionaries, who save them from their barbarism.

This attitude to black people in religion is a modern construction: black people were active in the Christian church long before the West African slave trade and the colonisation of Africa.

III. 6. The coronation of Pope Livi

This illustration from about 1425 shows an African bishop among those officiating at the ceremony. Many paintings and drawings of the period show black priests and knights and black people in other walks of life. Clearly, black people were active in Europe before the 'discovery' of America and the subsequent West African slave trade which followed.

III. 7. The disputation between St Erasmus and St Maurice

This painting by Mathias Grüenwald records the presence of black African leaders among the Christians in the period before the Crusades.

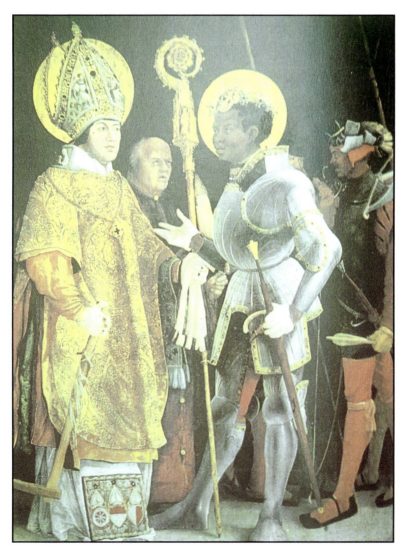

III. 8. The Martyrdom of St George

In this painting by Altricero, the importance of black people among the Muslim forces is evident. The African head emblem on the armour of the chief presiding officer was a device used by European artists to associate African people with the Muslim World. It was based on the belief that the Prophet Mohammed was of African origin and also on the fact that once the Muslims conquered North Africa, many Africans fought in their armies.

III. 9. The worship of Isis

Black people were active in the establishment of religions long before the birth of Mohammed or Jesus Christ.

This painting, uncovered at Pompeii, shows black religious leaders active in the worship of Isis, which had a large following in Rome, from before the birth of Christ until Christianity became the official religion of the Roman Empire.

III. 10. Isis with the infant Horus

This image was an established Egyptian motif. The Mother/Goddess and her son, with her husband Orisis beside her, was the earliest known 'Holy Family' of any religion.

After Christianity received its official sanction under the Emperor Constantine, the Virgin Mary and the infant Jesus — The Madonna of the Roman Christian Church — was promoted to assist in converting the followers of the Mother Goddess to the Christian faith.

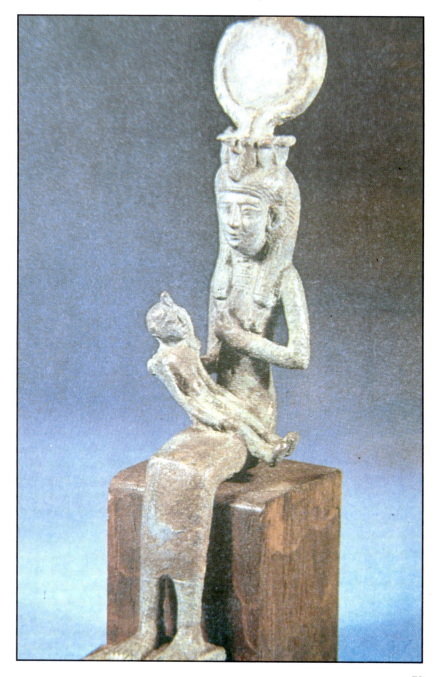

III. 11. The black Madonna of Einsiedeln

One of the many still existing Black Madonnas. It is likely that the images were all at first black. But as Northern Europeans began to dominate the faith, the images became European. There are records of Black Madonnas being destroyed by Christian zealots and others painted over in European flesh colour.

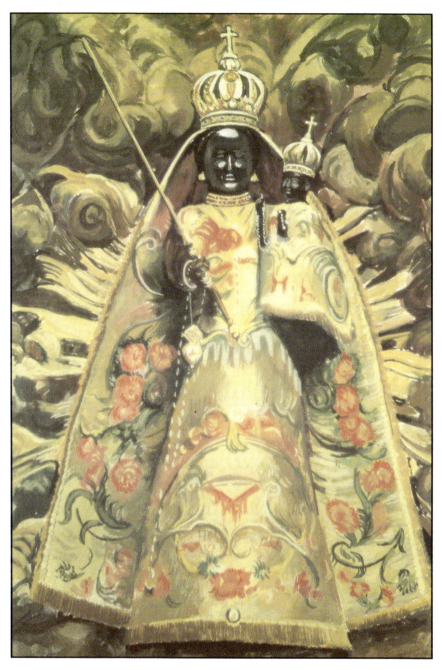

III. 12. Amenhotep IV or Akenaten

Egypt is also the source of the belief in one God or monotheism. The first known establishment of this religious belief was by the 'Heretic King' of the Eighteenth Dynasty of Egypt.

He changed his name to Akenaten in order to identify himself with the Sun God, Aten whom he claimed to be the only God. He himself was the earthly representative of that divine power. In his 'Hymn to Aten' are the lines 'There is no other that knoweth thee save thy son Akenaten'. According to Akenaten, Aten was a universal god. Unlike other Egyptian religious symbolism of their deities, there are no personifications or animal representations of Aten. Instead, the god is represented by a disc with rays ending in hands, which bestow blessings or hold the Ankh, the symbol of life.

III. 13. The Egyptian priest Pay and his Nubian wife

This Egyptian drawing shows a priest and his Nubian wife and relates to a story told by the Greek historian Herodotus. According to the story, the Oracles at Delphi and Dodona in Greece were set up by two black doves that flew over the water from Egypt.

This complements a story told in Egypt about two black priestesses who were stolen from a temple by Phoenician sailors and sold to the Greeks.

In Egypt the priesthood was hereditary and since — as this drawing proves — priests might have Nubian wives, black priestesses can be explained. The story is further confirmed by the image of a black man on small silver coin from Delphi. Some historians believe this represents Delphenes, the son of Melaina, who established the 'Oracle'. Others say that the image on the coin represents Aesop, the teller of the fables, who met his death on that Island.

III. 14. Aesop

*In this Greek drawing we see that Aesop is a black man.
He began his life in Greece as a slave but his wit and intelligence
earned favour with his master who became a friend and set him
free. During his lifetime Aesop became renowned in Greece and
his work influenced many of the later philosophers. An honest and
outspoken man, he was thrown from a cliff to his death on the
island of Delphi by locals he had offended by his
disparagement of Delphi.*

*Herodotus and Homer credited the Egyptians for being the first
in many human endeavours, particularly in the fields of
religion and medicine.*

III. 15. Imhotep

In Egypt the priest was also the physician and this combination reached a peak in the person of Imhotep.

Imhotep was a High Priest in the reign of King Djoser, Third Dynasty. He is described as an architect — he designed the Step Pyramid— and as astronomer, sage, scribe, magician and physician.

As a physician, he understood the circulation of the blood, 4,000 years before this knowledge was 're-discovered' by doctors in Europe. It was he who set up the tradition of healing which led to Homer's observation that 'In Egypt the men are more skilled in medicine than any of human kind'. After his death, Imhotep was worshipped as a God.

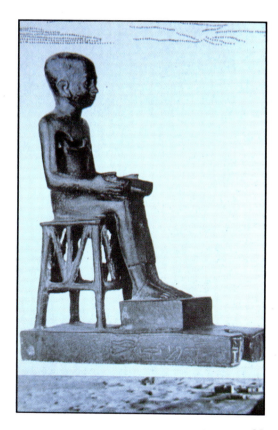

III. 16. The Eye of Horus

A stylised symbol based on the 'Eye of Horus' is used on prescriptions even today.

The Eye of Horus is an Egyptian symbol associated with healing. It relates to the story of the struggle between Horus and his evil Uncle Seth. Horus was wounded in the eye and it required the healing powers of Isis to repair the injury. This joining of religion and medicine from the earliest period of Western civilisation was based on the North Eastern corner of Africa and its influence spread out in every direction.

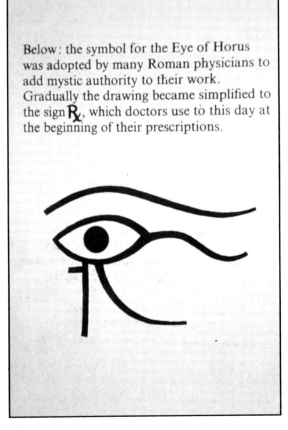

Below: the symbol for the Eye of Horus was adopted by many Roman physicians to add mystic authority to their work. Gradually the drawing became simplified to the sign ℞, which doctors use to this day at the beginning of their prescriptions.

SECTION THREE

Religion and the role of Black people

Teachers' Notes

In 1985 the Reverend Wilfred Woods was ordained as Bishop of Croydon and became the first black Bishop in the Church of England. There had been little scope for the progress of black people in the Church of England. It had broken away from the Church of Rome about the time of the birth of Queen Elizabeth and it was towards the end of her reign that Britain entered the West African slave trade.

Throughout the period of black enslavement, the established church had justified the practice, basing its position on Leviticus 25-44. 'Thy bondmen and bondmaids shall be the heathen that are around you, of them shall ye buy bondmen and bondmaids'. To which was later added the idea that it was the destiny of black people to be slaves because they were 'the children of Ham', so ordained to be hewers of wood and carriers of water.

It was the non-conformist sects such as Quakers and Baptists and later, Methodists who believed in the common brotherhood of all humanity, that first accepted black slaves into the Protestant Churches. Catholics had always baptised their slaves and allowed them to attend church on Sunday but did not encourage the idea that this entitled the slaves to freedom.

However, many African slaves had been Muslims before being taken into Christian captivity, and were accustomed to the Muslim tradition that the converted slave was entitled to freedom. The result was that many black runaway slaves in England had themselves baptised and sometimes petitioned for their freedom through the courts on those grounds.

In 1749 Chief Justice Holt ruled that slaves became free by setting foot on English soil — basing his judgement on the earlier concept that 'the air of England was too pure for slaves to breathe'. But Holt's ruling was promptly overturned by Yorke and Talbot, who ruled that neither residence in England nor baptism into the Christian religion made slaves exempt from the condition of slavery.[1]

In the colonies, Quakers and Baptists continued to convert black slaves and to oppose slavery. During periods of unrest, the churches were often the only place where black people could assemble in safety. The black churches which developed out of that situation were therefore closely linked to the struggle for freedom and identity.

Two of Jamaica's national heroes were Baptist Ministers who tried to bring the Christian teaching into the social arena — Sam Sharpe and Paul Bogle. Meanwhile in America, Quakers and Baptists were active in the setting up and running of the 'Underground Railway' by which many slaves were to escape from captivity in the Southern States to freedom in Northern States and escape to Canada.

So there has always been a high proportion of religious people in the organisations working for the advancement of black people, and black church-men have often taken the lead in trying to gain civil rights for their people — for example Reverend Martin Luther King and Archbishop Desmond Tutu.

In Catholic countries, notably in Brazil and Haiti, African people have often merged the religious practices of their ancestors with the Christian faith and have religious practices that differ from those of the orthodox church of Rome.

The Black Protestant churches of the English speaking world have also developed distinctive practices in the style of sermons and in the use of music and rhythm at services. There is a wide overflow into the field of popular music, and there are ever- increasing moves to bring black 'Gospel' music into general worship.

Many popular contemporary black singers started their careers in church choirs, and many of the messages of black liberation are carried in popular music. The 'Motown' label carries the message of black freedom and liberation, while the 'Reggae' scene, popularised by Bob Marley, is laced with ideas of black freedom and the Rastafarian religion.

Modern Christianity in Africa is characterised by the image of the white missionary bringing civilisation and true religion to the heathen blacks. It is often linked to racist notions, caricatured by the missionary in a large pot, about to be cooked by black cannibals.

The ancestral shrines of Africa with their carvings and monuments are seen as examples of primitive paganism, yet in practice most African religions have a common belief in 'the power without beginning' or some other creative force which is not very different from the Christian idea of God.[2]

Areas of Africa were practising Christianity before the people of Northern Europe were converted to the faith. Roman North Africa was the major stronghold of Christianity during the period of the persecutions and it was in Africa that many of the early martyrs met their death or, as they saw it, their God. St Cyprian and the Christian writer Tertullian were both natives of Africa and up to 411 Donatist Bishops from Africa amounted to 279, against 286 from Italy and France combined. No known records exist to tell us how many of these North African Christians were black, but in that part of the world, where the population seems always to have been mixed, it would be very unlikely that some were not of African heritage.

In East Africa, the Nubians were converted to Christianity in 543 by missionaries from Byzantium sent by Theodora, the wife of the Emperor Justinian, who favoured the Monophysite schism. In spite of the Muslim invasion in 642, most remained Christians.[3]

Some of these black Christians took part in the Crusades, and there are records of the Muslim leader, Saladin, when based in the Middle East, giving warnings to armies from Europe and their 'allies in the South'.

Until the fifteenth and even sixteenth century, illustrations and paintings show black priests e.g. in *The Marriage at Cana* by Veronese. Nevertheless the Crusades are generally portrayed in terms of Europe fighting to protect the truth and rightiousness against the heathen Muslims with their black supporters and even leaders (see Section II).

For a while, the conflicting images of the black as partner and the black as enemy persisted and this is reflected in the Coats of Arms of many prominent European families, where a black head may be in the dominant position. In other families, blacks are portrayed chained, blindfolded or in servile positions. Families may explain the black or Moor's Head emblem on their Coats of Arms as signifying that their ancestors fought against the Moors in Spain, but why then is the symbol in a dominant position?[4]

89

The influence of Africans upon the religions of the Mediterranean has a long history which goes back to the religious practices of Egypt.

Many Romans took up the worship of Isis after their occupation of Egypt under Julius Ceasar and paintings based on the ceremonies have been uncovered at Pompeii and Herculanium. But the religion is much older and its practice had been marked by the Greek historian Herodotus as widespread on the Northern shores of the African continent.

Isis was the female deity of Ancient Egypt, and with her husband Orisis and her son Horus, made up the first 'Holy Family' of any religion. Isis was the most important of the three and represented fertility, birth, death and resurrection. In the art works of Egypt she is often shown with the infant Horus on her lap — the original Madonna and Child. She wears a crown comprised of a disc, representing the Moon, supported by the two horns of a cow. She is also sometimes shown as a cow with the disc between its horns. In this form, she is called Hather. In Egyptian cosmology, the Universe was represented as a cow — possibly the origin of the concept of the Milky Way.

The Mother Goddess was worshipped in most societies around the Mediterranean: as Ishtar in Syria, Astarte in Phoenecia, Kybele in Asia Minor, Magna Mater in Rome. In Greece her various aspects were given separate identities: Hera, Athena, Aphrodite, Demeter. Kali, the goddess of the Hindu religion also has some of her attributes.[5]

In the Judeo/Christian bible, the Mother Goddess is first shown as in opposition to the male Jehovah, the God of Israel. Exodus tells how Moses returns to his people with the Ten Commandments, to find that they have erected a Golden Calf to worship. Why it should be a Golden Calf is not explained in the Bible, but these were the Jews who had fled Egypt — where Hathor was worshipped. Several stories in Egypt tell of the erection of golden statues of cows. Later, the Bible relates the prophet Jeremiah's anger at the Israelites' 'returning to the worship of Astarte'.[6] Thus it appears that for a time in the early formation of the Jewish faith, people fluctuated between the worship of the Mother Goddess and the male Jehovah. This may explain why the elements of the cow came to be identified with the Evil One, Satan, said in that faith to possess horns, cloven feet and a tail.

In early Christianity, the Church itself assumed the role of the Mother Goddess and became Mother Church. In the words of Clement of Alexandria: 'undefiled as a virgin and loving as a mother... nursing her children with holy milk, because the Word was milk'. And to St Augustine the Church was Christ's

Bride. It was not until AD 431 that the Council of Ephesus conferred upon Mary the right to the title 'Theotokos' or 'God Bearer': Mother of God.

As the Christian Church spread, many pagans were converted from the worship of the Mother Goddess and Mary, Mother of Christ, acquired her attributes.[7] Pagan festivals were taken into the Christian calendar with only minimal changes in their form. Their meaning, explained now by Christian theology, is still evident in the prayers/chant of the Roman Catholic Rosary. The first part is: 'Hail Mary... blessed art thou among women and blessed is the fruit of thy womb, Jesus' (fertility); the second is 'Holy Mary, Mother of God, pray for us sinners now and at the hour of our death' (death). Mary is still associated with birth, fertility and death but the power of resurrection is passed to her son, Jesus.

Images of the Mother Goddess sometimes show her as an African woman and there are even some Greek and Roman statues that show her as black. Many of the Early Christian Madonnas were also black. Some were destroyed — at Luneville by a zealous missionary, at Chatillion-sur-Seine (burnt by revolutionists in 1793). Others were painted over in European flesh colour. More than forty such images survive in cathedrals and churches in Italy, Spain, France, Switzerland, Hungary and Russia.[8]

The intensity with which the mother goddess was worshipped in southern Europe, whether in the form of Isis, Astarte, Demeter, Artemis or any other name, is echoed by the veneration of the Christian Madonna in this region to this day.

Even more importantly, the concept of monotheism — the belief in one god — was first practised in Egypt by the negroid Pharaoh Amenhotep IV, who changed his name to Akenanten and built a new place of worship to the Sun God, Aten, away from the centre of the worship of Amen at Thebes.He proclaimed that Aten was not only the sole god of the Egyptians, but of all humanity. The Egyptians symbolised their deities in the form of animals, but Aten was never portrayed in this way. Nor were there representations in animal form - except for human hands shown at the end of rays extending from the Sun.

Akenaten ruled at the time when the Israelites are said to have left Egypt, and his influence on their concept of God should not be overlooked. Furthermore, Akenaten influenced the form of language and hymns in praise of God.

There is further evidence of the activities of black people in the religions of the Mediterranean cultures. A painting in the Temple of Bel reveals black priests of the official cult practiced by the Parthians at Dura-Europa; it shows a black priest officiating at the ceremony attended by the Konon family, whose names are written in Greek. The painting dates from about 180 AD and provides no clues to precisely what religion was being observed.

In Greece, legend has it that the Oracle at the Temple of Apollo on the island of Delphi was set up by one of two black priestesses stolen from a temple in Egypt by Phoenician sailors and sold to the Greeks and that the other established the Oracle at Dodona.

The priests of Egypt were also the Physicians. Medical treatment apparently involved prescriptions of herbs and chemicals, combined with incantations and religious observance. It was, nevertheless, the most effective healing practice of the time. The tradition was established in the early period of dynastic Egypt and brought to prominence by the scribe, Imhotep from the period of King Djoser. He is said to be 'the first physician to stand out from the mist of time'. The inscription on a statue in his honour at Philae reads:

> Chancellor of the King of Lower Egypt. Chief under the King of Upper Egypt. Administrator of the Great Mansion. Hereditary Noble. Heliopolitan High Priest Imhotep.

He was sage, scribe, architect (of the Step Pyramid), astronomer and magician. He as also a physician, with an understanding of the blood circulatory system— 4000 years before its 'discovery' in Europe. Records show that he coined the phrase 'eat, drink and be merry for tomorrow ye shall die', attributed to St Paul in the New Testament.

The tradition set up by Imhotep earned the Egyptians their reputation for healing. In the words of Homer: 'in Egypt men are more skilled in medicine than any of human kind'.

Imhotep was worshipped as a god after his death and was identified by early Christians with the Prince of Peace. According to archaeologist Gerald Massey, the image of Imhotep was represented in the form of a black child. The Franciscan Order still keep an image of a black child, which is taken to visit the sick.[9]

To this day the influence of the Egyptians in the field of medicine is acknowledged by doctors: a stylised representation of the Egyptian symbol of healing, the *Eye of Horus,* appears at the top of prescriptions.

North Africa and the Muslim world have helped to maintain and develop medicine and other disciplines such as philosophy and astronomy. For several centuries they were the leading scientists, technologists and collectors of knowledge. Throughout the Dark Ages of Europe it was the Muslims who preserved and expanded human knowledge in their universities. Christians only discovered their capacity to cure and heal during the Crusades. In Muslim Spain, Christians eventually began to translate Arabic texts into European languages.[10] This practice became an industry in Toledo in the 12th century, when Archbishop Raymond of that town, which by then had been taken over by the Christians, set up a school of translators, and the great literary and scholarly works of the Ancient World, which had been gathered and expanded by the Muslims, were translated into European languages. That flow of knowledge fuelled the European Renaissance.

Scholars whose works were translated included Aristotle, Hippocrates, Geber, Appollonius, Ptolemy and Aesop.

SECTION FOUR

The Centuries of struggle

This book has dealt extensively with the interactions of African people and Europeans, both across the Mediterranean and across the Atlantic. We have seen how the trans-Atlantic trade in slaves changed the relationship, consigning Africans to a subordinate position. We have also considered the resistance of some who would not conform and others who struggled to make the best of the conditions under which they had to live.

Section 4 traces the progress of that struggle and its impact on the people of Africa. It looks at the traditions of Africa before the period of European domination and at African adaptation to the European presence and briefly outlines the struggles for liberation from colonial rule.

IV. 1: Marcus Garvey

One of the most influential black leaders to emerge early in the 20th century was Marcus Garvey, who started the Universal Negro Improvement Association in Jamaica in 1914. The Association advocated world wide self-government for black people, self-help economic projects, cultural activities and organised protest against racial discrimination.

Garvey moved to the USA in 1916 and continued to preach and practice his doctrine among the oppressed blacks. The authorities, concerned by his message, imprisoned and deported him. He continued his work in Jamaica and then moved to England where he became part of the Pan-African movement.

The overtly racist basis of World War II, which began before Garvey died, created the right conditions for his ideas to flourish after the war, both in the New World and in Africa.

IV. 2. The Reverend Martin Luther King

In America the first and probably the most influential black leader to attract world wide attention was Martin Luther King.

Head of the Southern Christian Leadership Conference, his ideas differed from those of Marcus Garvey. He sought not self-government for black people but their integration as respected citizens into the cultural, economic, educational and social life of a single society.

To those ends, he led the non-violent struggle against the segregation laws existing in many states and protested against the continued oppression of his people by such organisations as the Ku Klux Klan and individuals who advocated the superiority of white people.

IV. 3. Francis Kwame Nkrumah

The second World War also influenced the process of the decolonisation of Africa. In the Gold Coast, a new era of African liberation commenced with the emergence of such leaders as Nkrumah.

Nkrumah led the struggle for the liberation of his country from British rule, and on gaining Independence renamed it Ghana, after an older Kingdom which had existed to the North several centuries before.

Nkrumah had been active in the Pan-African movement in Britain and the United States and returned to Africa when invited to become the secretary of the United Gold Coast Convention. In an incident now called 'the flurry at the crossroads', violence erupted involving men who had been soldiers during the Second World War; Nkrumah and five others were arrested for promoting a 'communist plot'. Following an official enquiry they were released, but Nkrumah was dismissed by the UGCC. He then formed his own party, The Convention Peoples Party, at the head of which he led Ghana to independence.

The liberation of Ghana from colonial rule set the pattern for the decolonisation of Africa.

Fig. 33 — Kwame Nkrumah, first Prime Minister of Ghana.

99

IV. 4. Timbuktu, capital of Ancient Ghana

The renaming of Ghana symbolised the long history of the people of Africa before the colonisation of their continent by Europeans. Even during the period of the Crusades, trade across the Mediterranean had provided a route for the gold of Africa to Europe. The exchange of gold took place at Timbuktu. From there it was taken across the desert to Egypt, then the centre of the gold trade.

IV. 5. The Palette of Narmer

This plaque commemorates the joining of Upper and Lower Egypt under one ruler, Narmer (or Menes, as he is sometimes called). As ruler of Upper Egypt, Narmer conquered Lower Egypt and established the first large-scale unified state in known history.

The rulers or Pharaohs were seen as associates of the gods. This attitude to rulers is common to many societies in Africa. It has been assumed that this practice had spread from Egypt to other parts of Africa but it is possible that the customs of Egypt were adopted from African practice.

IV. 6. Map of Africa
(with 3 regions of Egypt marked out)

At the north east corner of the continent, Egypt is one of the oldest urban cultures in the world. Situated in the midst of a desert region, it depends on the waters of the Nile for its existence. It would be more correct to speak of the Nile Valley Civilisation of ancient times, because there were three social or political groupings: Lower Egypt, Upper Egypt and Nubia (See Section II).

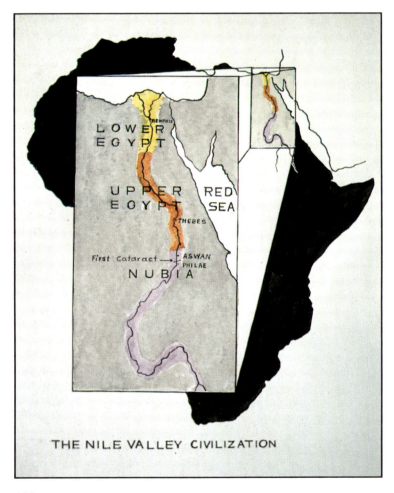

THE NILE VALLEY CIVILIZATION

IV. 7. Lion (Pharaoh) and Nubian

United Egypt exerted its military might over its southern neighbour and forced the Nubians to pay tribute to the Pharaohs. In this drawing, the ruler of Egypt is symbolised as a Lion biting the head of the Nubian. This is possibly the oldest representation of the black man as a victim. Later works of art show alligators and other animals attacking black people.

IV. 8. Abu Simbel

Such was the relationship between Egypt and Nubia that many monuments considered to this day as Egyptian are actually in Nubia. The boundary was at the island of Elephantine, so the famous Temple of Isis at Philae and the colossal statues of Ramesses at Abu Simbel are in fact located in Nubia.

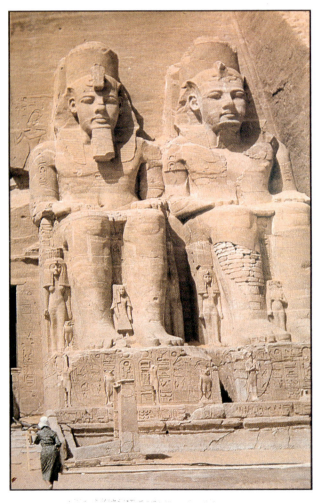

IV. 9. Pianky, Nubian conqueror of Egypt

For several centuries Nubia remained a vassal state of Egypt but by 1000 BC they had established their independence. In 750 BC, led by King Pianky they invaded and conquered Egypt and established the XXXV Dynasty.

In the face of the Assyrian invasion, they retreated to Meroe, where they continued to practice their independent culture, developing their own script, farming, smelting iron and trading with the people of the interior as well as along the Red Sea and the Eastern Coast of Africa, from where trade went as far as India.

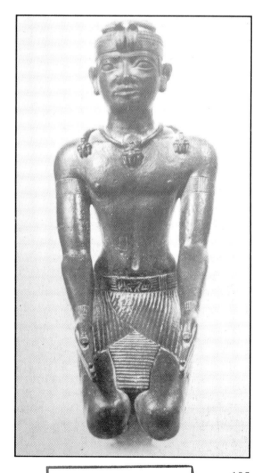

IV. 10. The remains of the Great Mosque at Kilwa

Now in ruins as the result of looting by the Portuguese early in the 16th century, this was the centre of worship for the Muslim natives and traders who visited the port. Kilwa was one of a network of trading ports on the eastern coast of Africa that stretched from Mogadishu in modern Somalia to Mozambique and included Malindi, Mombasa and Zanzibar. From these ports trade went as far as China and Indonesia.

IV. 11. Great Zimbabwe

The trade depended on the supply of ivory, leather, gold and other products from the interior. In the 13th century this supply was controlled by the rulers of the Karanga Clan, part of the Rowzi people. The centre of power was located at the royal enclosures or Zimbabwe, the most impressive being Great Zimbabwe (see section II). On gaining liberation from British rule, the former colony of Rhodesia was re-named Zimbabwe.

IV. 12. Kano and Katsina

The gold from Timbuktu lost its importance in world trade after the European occupation of central America but the trade across the desert continued. The towns of Kano and Katsina supplied trade goods, which were carried north to the Mediterranean shore.

IV. 13. Benin the Ashanti

As trade in slaves developed along the West Coast of Africa, the rulers of Benin, Ashanti and Dahoney were among those who protected themselves by acting as middle men, selling others rather than being sold.

IV. 14. The Kalabari

The Kalabari were fishermen of the Niger Delta. They turned to slave trading when the opportunity arose and, when the slave-trade was abolished, to dealing in palm oil. The trade in palm oil was later taken over by British traders, helped by the British Navy.

Jaja

FEW p
the stoi
Opubo.
Jaja wa
ca, Brit
bean.

Jaja (King Ja
Pebble) was bor
in the Igbo regio
ern Nigeria. S
from his parer
passed his early
the service of a N
trading house.

While still in
20s he establishe
transport busine
ping palm-olive
Nigerian interior
pean buyers on
By 1870 he had
fortune and sec
throne of the "C
town of Opuh
proved an excell
of state, winr
admiration of F
and Africans ali

Then as now, r
rials command
price in Europe I

IV. 15. The Ambassador from the Congo

In the sixteenth century the rulers of the Congo tried to stop the trade in slaves from their country. This proved to be impossible and by the 17th century they too were forced to deal in slaves. It is indicative of the level of the operation that they sent ambassadors to Portugal and Brazil to supervise their interests.

IV. 16. Shaka — The Zulu

*The settlement of Europeans on the southern tip of Africa in the
18th century, and their gradual spread into the interior, brought
about changes among the African tribes. Some leaders recognised
the need for uniting the tribes against the foreign intruders. At first
they formed two large groups, one of which was
led by Dingiswayo.*

*Shaka, one of King Dingiswayo's followers, became leader of a
small community of Zulus. On the death of Dingiswayo, Shaka
took control of the tribal grouping, with his own tribe at the
centre. With this power base he set out to unite the tribes of
Southern Africa by force.*

The mighty Shaka, founder of the Zulu nation. This
drawing by James Saunders King is the only authentic
portrait of the first Zulu King.

IV. 17. Livingstone and Stanley

The northward spread of Europeans from South Africa was much influenced by Livingstone, Stanley and Rhodes. A large central area was secured as British colonies, the Portuguese having already occupied Mozambique in the East and Angola in the West.

IV. 18. The Mau Mau and Jomo Kenyetta

The British colonists resisted all attempts at peaceful liberation. The people of the area resorted ultimately to guerrilla warfare, following the pattern set earlier in Kenya, where the colonists had also resisted political agreement to end colonial rule.

The men of the Kikuyu then formed themselves into a military secret society called the Mau Mau and waged a war of attrition against the settlers. When Jomo Kenyatta was released from prison, agreement was reached for the independence of Kenya under his leadership. `

IV. 19. Robert Mugabe

Throughout the 1960s the Portuguese colonies of Angola and Mozambique were in a state of civil war. The British gave up many of their colonies by peaceful negotiation, but the last of these, Southern Rhodesia, refused to hand over to the African population. The white government issued a Unilateral Declaration of Independence, which resulted in guerrilla warfare and, ultimately, acceptance of African rule under Robert Mugabe. The country was renamed Zimbabwe.

IV. 20. Nelson Mandela

Mandela has become the focus of the struggle to liberate South Africa from its present rulers with their discriminatory policy of apartheid. As leader of the African National Congress, Mandela approved the formation of an armed wing of the Congress, Umkonto Wa Sizwe (The Spear of the Nation).

The township revolt of 1962 resulted in 83 Africans shot dead and 365 wounded at Sharpville and Langa. Mandela was arrested along with the high command of the armed wing. At his trial in 1963, Mandela refused to renounce the use of force as a means of liberation. He was sentenced to life imprisonment, along with other members of the ANC executive. They were released after twentyseven years during which continued pressure was put on the government by both internal and external agencies, and recognised as the representative body for the African people to negotiate with the Afrikanaans government towards majority rule.

SECTION FOUR

The Centuries of struggle

Teachers' notes

The struggle against slavery led to the formation of black organisations dedicated to the liberation and advancement of black people at the West. Most prominent in the United States were the Urban League and the National Association for the Advancement of Coloured People. Because the Black Churches were the only form of Black organisation permitted, there was always a high proportion of religious people among their personnel.

Black people were now free but were not educated or regarded as capable as their white countrymen. The onus was on them to get themselves educated and to 'prove' their capability. There was, in reality, no acceptance, except on a token level and education and training was denied to the majority. The segregation of services and amenities further emphasised the division and separation of the society.

The system operated differently in the English-speaking countries of the Caribbean. There black people were in the majority and a high proportion of the wealth of the colonies belonged either to absentee white landowners or to the few white settlers who had remained after the abolition of slavery and their cousins of varying degrees of racial mixture. The possession of wealth and position was often in inverse proportion to the degree of pigmentation.

Marcus Garvey

In 1914 Marcus Garvey launched his struggle against the existing system. Like Karl Marx, he recognised the relationship between economy and the control of power but as mitigated by colour and culture. It was the modes and customs of Europe (or white society) which were accepted and respected while those of Africa were subject to disapproval and rejection. This had been underwritten by the scientific racism of the Victorian era which still prevailed: 'Social Darwinism', or an extension of Darwin's theory of evolution to humankind, with 'Negroid' people lower on the scale than 'Caucasians'. Garvey tried to counter this view by advocating the setting up of a black power system independent of white society. Black people would set up their own system of economy, form black armies and establish shipping companies.

When he took his ideas to the United States, he soon gained a large following. This alarmed the white authorities, and Garvey was arrested on false charges of fraud and embezzlement related to the money and organisations which he controlled, including the Black Star Shipping Company he had established.[1]

He was deported back to Jamaica where he formed the People's Political Party in 1929. But because voting rights were restricted to people with property or a relatively high income, many of his followers were not qualified to vote and he failed to gain a seat in the national elections.

He migrated to England in the 1930s and continued his activities, speaking in halls and at Hyde Park. With others whose names are now synonymous with the struggle for liberation: Kwame Nkrumah, Jomo Kenyatta, Eric Williams, C.L.R. James and Patrice Lumumba, he spearheaded the Pan African movement which reached its peak with a conference at Manchester in 1945. This movement, began as a New World defence of coloured people from the pressures of white-dominated society, and became a training school for the future leaders of what was then colonial Africa, particularly those regions controlled by the British.

Garvey did not live to see the outcome of his ideas. Except for a period in Canada, helping to establish a school of philosophy, he spent the rest of his life in England, where he died in 1940. His body was returned to Jamaica in 1964 and buried in the National Heroes Park.

In recent years, disclosures made about the Federal Bureau of Investigation in the USA have revealed that he had been unjustly accused and imprisoned there and efforts have been made by the Government of Jamaica to have his conviction removed from the records.

120

Black soldiers, white wars

The second World War was followed by East/West confrontation, and for Americans the first area of conflict was Korea. Once more, many black soldiers were involved. While they were fighting for the American supremacy, they began to see the colonies of Africa liberating themselves from their colonial masters. *Ebony* magazine printed an editorial proclaiming that while for years 'the sun had not set on the British Empire' it now stood at 'high noon' over Asia and beckoned the dawn of a New Africa. When, *Ebony* asked, would it be American blacks who were liberated from oppression?

There had already been movements for the desegregation of schools in Alabama, which had to be carried out with the protection of the National Guard, when Reverend Martin Luther King led a boycott of the buses, after Rosa Parkes rebelled against the segregation that meant that blacks could sit only at the back. The struggle grew and spread to the campaign for the de-segregation of lunch counters in the Southern States and for voting rights. Reverend King led the famous march from Selma to Montgomery in 1965. By then others had rebelled against the passive model of resistance based on the philosophy of Mahatma Gandhi. Stokley Carmichael, now known as Kwame Ture, led the cry of Black Power and the Black Muslims advocated the partitioning of the United States, to allow for the formation of free black states.

Soldiers returning from Vietnam took up arms once more, to fight for their own freedom in the country for which they had gone to war. They formed organisations such as the Black Panthers, but the establishment exercised its greater capacity for violence and most of the Panthers were killed.

Martin Luther King's influence and reputation grew and in 1964 he was awarded the Nobel Prize for Peace. In 1968 he delivered his famous speech to a massive crowd in Washington, with the recurring theme 'I have a dream'. Weeks later he was assassinated. But his ideas and the organisation he set in motion continue to influence world thought.

The new breed of leaders, trained in the Pan-African school of thought which flourished from early in the 20th century, returned to Africa after World War II and found responsive audiences among their people.

Kwame Nkrumah was called to the Gold Coast following his work at the Pan-African Conference in Manchester, the high point of his ten years of study in England and America.[2] He was made Secretary of the United Gold Coast Convention. In 1948 violence broke out in the Gold Coast, sparked off by soldiers home from the War. It ended in riots in which the main targets were the European trading companies and their property.

Not unreasonably, men who had fought to free Ethiopia, Burma, India and France from foreign domination, could not be restrained from advocating and taking action for the same purpose in their homeland.

Nkrumah and five others were arrested for promoting a 'communist plot' and although they were released after an official inquiry, Nkrumah was dismissed by the UGCC. He formed his own convention, the People's Party and with it behind him, promoted a programme of 'positive action'. (i.e. strikes and boycotts) for immediate self-government. On achieving power he renamed the country Ghana, after the first West African State known to history.

The name of Ghana harks back to the African past (outlined in Chapter 1) and the relationship between the people of Europe and the people of Africa prior to the West African slave trade, when Timbuktu flourished as a main source of gold.

The gold and wealth of black Africa had been used by the warrior, colonising, empire-building rulers of the Mediterranean region since the dawn of urban civilisation in the area. The first large-scale state was the Double Kingdom of Egypt, Upper and Lower, ruled by 'the Kings with two Crowns.' The conquest of Lower by Upper Egypt was recorded on a stone slab, 'The Palette of Narmer', showing the victorious ruler wearing the crown of Upper Egypt on one side and of Lower Egypt on the other. Subsequent representations of Egyptian rulers show them wearing the two crowns.[3]

Upper Egypt was mainly black while Lower Egypt was more mixed, with Berber people of North Africa, Semitic tribes of the Eastern Region and influences from Southern Europe.

Egyptian armies raided Nubia and made it a vassal state. Records from nearly three thousand years BC tell how the land of Nubia was hacked to pieces; how 7000 men and women were taken, as well as 200,000 cattle and sheep.[4] Later wall paintings show Nubians presenting the Pharaohs with cattle, giraffe, monkey, animal skins, gold and slaves. By about 2000 BC the Nubians were under Egyptian military control. But domination was not complete. Many Nubians served in the Egyptian armies and as priests and officials, and some even became rulers (see chapter 2). Many of the ancient monuments regarded as Egyptian were actually located above the first cataract i.e. in Nubia.

The area is now flooded by the High Dam at Aswan. Some idea of the many monuments — virtually one vast out-door museum — can be gathered from the books and records made by those involved in the UNESCO project of the 1960s to save the monuments from the rising water. They include the Colossal images of Ramesses II and the Roman temple of Isis on the island of Philae.

Before the invasions of Egypt by the Assyrians, Persians, Greeks and Romans, the Nubians had freed themselves from Egyptian rule, and had in turn conquered Egypt in 750 BC, ruling for about eighty years as the XXV Dynasty of Egypt.[5] In the face of the Assyrian invasion they retreated to Napata and later to Meroe where they established an independent society. Later they established diplomatic links with the rulers of Egypt and undertook joint projects such as building a temple at Dakka.

The Roman historian Starbo recorded Nubian contracts with the Romans. The Nubians developed their own society and their own script; they farmed the land, worked iron, mined gold and established trade along the Red Sea and the Coast of East Africa which reached as far as India. The Nubians were conquered by a desert tribe called the Blemmyes, who established their capital at Kalabasha. The Blemmyes were in turn defeated by the Noba King Silko.

Nubian trade on the Eastern Coast of Africa was part of the extensive trade routes across and around the Indian Ocean. The first recorded trade with the African coast was documented in Alexandria in about 110 AD in a pilot's book called the *Periplus of the Erythrean* and details towns from the Red Sea to Mozambique.[6] It lists the markets and ports of call, broken into daily runs, the people encountered, goods brought and sold, the prevailing winds at different seasons. The towns of Kenya and Tanganika — then called Azania — exported gold, rhinoceros horn, tortoise shells, ivory and palm oil. Despite the trade in ivory, rhinoceros and elephant still roamed the country in large numbers when the European settlers arrived in the 19th century. The organisers of the trade were the Arabs, who not only spoke the language of the natives and involved them in the trading activities but often inter-married with them.

Two hundred years after the *Periplus,* the *Geography* written by Claudius Ptolemy also tells of the trade, of the dark-skinned traders of the coast and of the gold which came from inland to the port of Sofala, south of the mouth of the Zambesi, in what is Zimbabwe.

When the Portuguese explorer Vasco de Gama first arrived on the east coast of Africa, he recorded that the people of the town expressed no surprise at seeing his ship and crew, only that they had come from the south. The ports were full of ships from India and China which were grander than his own and whose captains knew their way across oceans then unknown to Europeans. These ships brought Indian cloth, beads and swords, pottery and porcelain from China, stoneware from Siam.

The Europeans studied the town and the trade, then looted them, massacring the peaceful traders and destroying the buildings. They set up ports and garrisons to control the natives and occupied Goa in India as a base for that end of the trade. But without the goodwill of the people, the caravans which went inland for goods to be traded no longer operated and the trade collapsed. Many of the towns still flourish but ancient buildings such as the great Mosque at Kilwa are now in ruins and the coast of East Africa is littered with fragments of stoneware and the blue and white porcelain of the Ming Dynasty of China. In 1966 the Government of India occupied Goa and returned the region to Indian control.

Planters came to join the Portuguese traders in Mozambique and settlements were established by the late 16th century. These became more numerous until the area became a colony of Portugal, ending only with the war of liberation in the mid-20th century.

In the West of Africa, the trade in slaves and the reduction in the importance of the gold trade from Timbuktu reduced the African people to degradation and the region to poverty.

By 1492 the Songhai had taken control of Mali from the Mandingo rulers under the leadership of Sonni Ali. Later, during the reign of Askia Mohammed, records of that state reached European Christians through the works of Leo Africanus, a Muslim scholar captured by Christians and sold as a slave in Italy.

The final blow to the glory of Timbuktu came in 1598 when the ruler of Morocco sent an army equipped with firearms against the people of Songhai who were armed only with spears and swords. The frightened natives fled before the invaders and contributed to the confusion which European traders then exploited to establish the West African slave trade.

African trade with the North continued. Goods were sold to Morocco and Tunisia from towns in the South of the desert in the Hausa states of Kano and Katsina. The leather goods from these towns even reached Europe— wrongly described as Moroccan leather.

To the south west were the Yoruba states of Ife, Benin and Oyo. Benin was a walled city. Early travellers recorded that it was twenty six miles in circumference, with main streets four miles long. Its ruler was treated in the manner of the god-kings of Africa and seen by his people once a year when he went on a 'public progress' round the outside of his palace, riding on horseback and accompanied by nobles and musicians.[8] The king controlled all craft work in precious metal and the casting of images in bronze, work which is among the most elaborate and exquisite to come out of Africa (see Section 1).

The rulers of Benin were among those who joined in the slave trade, controlling the flow of slaves from their region. The Ashanti tribes (today's Ghana) did likewise, taking gold and slaves northwards to Timbuktu. As the trade on the southern coast developed, they turned their attention in that direction and slaves became more profitable than gold. Early in the sixteenth century the Portuguese were taking up to fifteen ship-loads of slaves from the area each year. For over three hundred years the Europeans trading in these 'commodities' knew only that they came from 'the bush', but knew nothing of what lay behind the bush.

It was not until 1817 that T.E. Bowdich was instructed to make contact with the Ashanti by his employers, the British West African Company. He arrived at Kumasi, a city of 15000 people, wearing expensive clothing and golden ornaments. By then, however, people in England had come to perceive Africans as poor, naked miserable savages and Bowdich's description of the Ashanti and their city was mocked and rejected.[9]

Over fifty years later, the British went to war against the Ashanti, now ruled by a new Ashantehene (king) named Kori Karikari. Records of the Ashanti Wars include accounts of a mysterious Golden Stool in which the power of the Ashantehene was vested. The Golden Stool had descended from heaven into the keeping of the first ruler. Its symbolic power was so great that when Sir Frederick Hodson, Governor of the Gold Coast, went to Kumasi in 1900, he demanded:

> Where is the Golden Stool? Why am I not sitting on the Golden Stool at this moment? I am the representative of paramount power: Why have you relegated me to this chair? Why did you not take the opportunity of my coming to Kumasi to bring the Golden Stool and give it to me to sit upon?

The chiefs took his questions as an insult, and subjected the Governor's party to a humiliating siege. The Governor did not know that no human being had ever sat upon the Golden Stool, and to do so would have been as great a sacrilege as eating a plate of Holy Bread for breakfast would be to a Roman Catholic.

A British force of 1044 British soldiers and 449 African troops, led by 118 officers attacked Kumasi in February 1874. Their weapons were far superior to those of the Ashanti. The town was occupied, looted and burned, although the Ashanti managed to smuggle large quantities of their wealth out of the town during the night. Of what remained some was stolen by individual British Army personnel. As late as 1976, a gold headband of Ashanti workmanship was sold in England for £6,000. According to the catalogue 'It had been stolen by Lieutenant Frederick Cowan of the Royal Welsh Fusiliers. He had found it in the King's dressing-room in the palace.' Thus did the treasures of Africa reach Europe. Many Ashanti objects are now in London's British Museum and Museum of Mankind.

Further along the coast of Africa in the Delta of the River Niger, the Kalabari fishermen turned from fishing to slave trading and, when that ended, to trading in palm oil.

In the European scramble for Africa, the British colonised the area and British trading houses took control of the trade, with the connivance of colonial customs officials and the assistance of the British Navy. When King Ja Ja of Apobo, a former slave who had risen to power, was appointed to lead negotiations during a boarding dispute, he made the mistake of trusting the British delegation and boarding a ship to carry on the discussions. As the talks progressed the ship sailed to the island of St Vincent in the West Indies, carrying Ja Ja to exile. Members of his family later joined him and on his death his body was returned to his homeland, but some of his descendants still live in St Vincent and neighbouring islands.

In the Congo, rulers tried to stop the sale of people from their territory, but eventually succumbed to the slave trade. By the end of the seventeenth century they were sending Ambassadors to Portugal and Brazil to supervise their interest.[10] A drawing of the period shows Dutch Traders kneeling before the king of the Congo, and a portrait of the Congolese Ambassador to Brazil now hangs in Sweden. In time, the Congolese were reduced to poverty and in the colonial era the Congo fell to the Belgians. Many atrocities were committed by the colonists in obtaining the wealth and later the labour of the Africans.[11]

During World War II many Belgians went to the Congo to escape the German advance. Very little preparation was made for the end of colonial rule and when the country was suddenly given independence in 1959 a civil war ensued, resulting in chaos and the killing of the first Prime Minister, Patrice Lumumba. Nevertheless the Belgians did not regain control over the country.

The disbelief which greeted T. Bowdich's description of Kumasi in 1817 indicates how common the view of Africans as naked barbarous savages had became among Europeans. Much more in tune with their perceptions and beliefs was the story told two decades later, about the Zulu leader Shaka.

CENTURIES OF STRUGGLE

The Zulus of today remember Shaka as the Father of their Nation and its greatest hero. The day of his death is commemorated annually and a monument in his honour stands on the site of his Kraal at Dukwaza.[12] He used his ability and an iron discipline to train his army. Prisoners of war could choose between death or swearing an oath of allegiance to him and his army. Shaka devised tactics for using his weapons to defeat European armies with their far more advanced weapons.

Dingiswayo, the Chief of the Mtherthwa clan to whom Shaka's mother belonged and with whom Shaka had grown up, had started to unite the tribes in his vicinity into a single group. Further north, the Ndawandwe clans were joining, through treaty or conquest, under the leadership of Chief Zwide. Both rulers had seen the necessity for strong groupings as a protection against the incursion of European settlers in Mozambique and the Cape.

As chief of the Zulus, Shaka began to subdue smaller surrounding peoples. He remained loyal to Dingiswayo but took power from his successors after he died. He then defeated the armies of Zwide and took the Ndwandwe into his fold by accepting vows of allegiance from those who would join him and putting to death those who would not. Marriages were arranged between members of the different peoples. By these means, he built the foundations of the Zulu nation, now the largest single African group in the Republic of South Africa.

Shaka's plan, the Mfecane (the crushing of several small tribes to form a single nation) was interpreted as an act of mindless slaughter by Europeans. It certainly drove some of the smaller tribes to flight at the advance of his ever-increasing force. Their flight into the domains of their neighbours led to a series of wars of encroachment that spread outward on every side. To the south this brought the Caffres (Kaffirs) into conflict with the European settlers and contributed to an atmosphere of hostility.

The story of Shaka was popularised in a book by Samuel Isaacs: *Travels and Adventure in Eastern Africa* (1836). Isaacs was one of the first of the British settlers near Port Elizabeth, under the leadership of Francis George Farewell. Another, Henry Francis Fynn, also began writing about Shaka and his followers. Isaacs advised Fynn to:

> Make them out as bloodthirsty as you can and endeavour to give an estimation of the number of people they had murdered during their reign, and describe the frivolous crimes people lose their lives for; introduce as many anecdotes relative to Shaka as you can; it tends to swell up the work and make it interesting.

127

The description of Shaka found in many British encyclopaedias appears to draw much from the speech given by the black character, Aaron, in Act V Scene 1 of Shakespeare's *Titus Andronicus*. It has been difficult to unravel the merging fact and fiction in British portrayals and perceptions of Shaka ever since.

The Zulu people were eventually overcome by the British and enabled the expansion of the colonies into Central Africa, associated with Livingstone, Stanley and Cecil Rhodes. Rhodes wanted to see Africa coloured red for Britain on the map, 'from Cairo to the Cape', but did not quite succeed.[13]

In the struggles for independence after the second World War, the Africans had to cope with colonial attitudes as well as power. The Africans of Kenya resorted to a protracted war of attrition led by the Kikuyu's secret society, the Mau Mau, which spread terror among the white settlers of the Highlands.[14] The Mau Mau were hunted down by the authorities, but many escaped into the bush and carried on the struggle, until Jomo Kenyatta was released from prison and a programme agreed for independence.

Other states were to gain their independence by more peaceful means. But the Portuguese colonies of Angola and Mozambique similarly gained their liberation only by means of long guerrilla wars. The people of Zimbabwe were forced to do the same after white colonists declared Unilateral Independence (UDI), rather than agree to terms leading to African majority rule, and Robert Mugabe was installed as president after a period of guerrilla warfare.

Further south, events after World War II took a different course. The first Europeans to settle in the Cape in 1652 were from Holland. By the eighteenth century tensions had grown, partly because of their use of local women and also because, while population increased, so did the number of the European settlers. The settlers' practice of making land enclosures as they moved inland, resulted in a series of clashes now known as the 'kaffir wars' and, indirectly, to the formation of the Zulu Nation under Shaka.

The first British settlers arrived in 1795 and in 1814 the Dutch ceded the Cape to Britain. After 1820 the British presence increased rapidly. Following the Abolition Act in England in 1833, slavery was outlawed in the colony and the Dutch settlers reacted against that British 'liberalism'. In protest, these Dutch farmers or 'Boers' began to migrate northwards in their ox- wagons, on their 'Great Trek'. In time their language had become a variant of Dutch and was officially recognised as 'Afrikaans' in 1905. The Boers first set up a republic at Natal in 1838, only to find themselves annexed by the British five years later. They moved on to found two provinces: the Orange Free State and the Transvaal.

The discovery of diamonds in the Free State and the gold reef in the Transvaal, combined with British empire-building led the British to dispossess the Boers of the Orange Free State. Until then the British had been on 'friendly' terms with the Zulus. But in 1879 they sent an army into Zululand, which was defeated at Isandhlwana by a Zulu army led by Chetshwayo. The victorious Zulu asked for a treaty but the British could not accept what they saw as their worst humiliation in Africa and were set on revenge. They brought in fresh troops, under new leadership and equipped with the newest military invention: the machine-gun. This force extracted revenge and put an end to the Zulu nation as a military power in the region.

The only opposition to remain was the Boer Republic of the Transvaal and the Anglo-Boer War began in 1899. The Boers used unconventional tactics of guerrilla warfare and the British reacted by placing large numbers of the Boer population, including women, in barbed-wire enclosures, creating the world's first concentration camps. The war lasted for three years and cost the British dear. Finally the British made a treaty with the Boers which was very different from that imposed upon the Zulus. Essentially, it allowed for both British and Boers to control and exploit the Africans, so institutionalising the supremacy of the whites over the blacks. The treaty of 1910 established the 'Union of South Africa', uniting the four vast provinces under a wholly white government. In 1913 the Land Act awarded 90% of the colony to the Europeans; the remaining 10% (later 13%) to be 'Native Reserves'. The rights of the native people to live and work in the Union was controlled by laws to 'regulate labour'.

Many Afrikaaner (Boer) leaders were imprisoned for supporting Hitler's Germany during World War II, but on their release after the war, their party won the 1948 (whites only) elections and assumed control of the country. The earlier laws formed the basis of their land distribution legislation, formalised into a system of *apartheid*. Africans were to live in their 'homelands', and the land division was based on supposed distribution of land after Shaka's Mfecane and the claims that the interior has been depopulated and then occupied by the migrating Boers. To live in white areas, Africans had to carry a work permit or Pass-book. Symbolic burnings of this Pass and other African resistance to policy was generally ignored. African political organisations were not recognised by the government and any sustained action resulted in leaders being persecuted or prosecuted. The African National Congress, composed of Africans, 'coloureds' (people of mixed race), and some white Liberals and Communists dedicated to the cause of democracy, was declared illegal, along with smaller resistance organisations. The government openly used force against Africans, most notoriously at Sharpville and Langa in 1962 where troops shot more than eighty Africans dead, and wounded three hundred and sixty five.

The ANC responded by approving the formation of their armed wing, *Umkonto Wa Sizwe* (the Spear of the Nation) before Nelson Mandela and other leaders of the ANC were arrested and charged with treason. At their trial in 1963 they refused to renounce the use of force as a means to liberation. They were sentenced to life imprisonment and the ANC was officially banned.

The struggle for liberation continued and other organisations were formed. One, the Black Consciousness Movement, was led by Steve Biko. Biko was arrested and, like dozens of other Africans who resisted the system, died in custody. The uprisings continued. Pupils boycotted schools when the Afrikaans language was made compulsory in the curriculum in 1976, leading to violence in Soweto, the largest of the African townships. Many children were shot by government troops; others fled the country, some joining camps in other African countries where they trained in use of weapons and the skills of guerrilla warfare. Beyond Africa, and notably in England, organisations such as the Anti-Apartheid movement drew attention to the policies of the South African government and the plight of the Africans. National boycotts of trade, arts and, most damagingly for the Afrikaaners, sport, became emulated by other countries in West and East. Black Americans took up the anti-apartheid cause.

These international pressures led to concessions by the South African government who had to deal with conflict with their own extreme right, dedicated to maintaining apartheid. The African people are also divided: some support the aims of the ANC; others, mainly Zulus, support the Inkatha movement formed by Zulu leader Buthelezi. Inkatha was originally set up as a national liberation movement in 1975 but the pragmatism of its leaders regarding apartheid has led to it increasingly being seen as an instrument of the white government. In 1979 it broke off contact with the exiled ANC.

The United Democratic Front, formed in 1983, identified closely with the ANC and have taken a back seat to the ANC in negotiations with the government since the release of Mandela in 1990. Clashes between the supporters of Inkatha, the UDF and the ANC have resulted in hundreds of deaths and it was recently disclosed that some of this violence was instigated by government officials. ANC supporters claim that the police and armed forces have not been impartial when dealing with the violence. Many Inkatha functions are now known to have been funded by government departments, but it remains a force to be reckoned with in the on-going negotiations. Buthelezi and Mandela have made appeals for an end to the violence, and both their organisations are involved in discussions with the government which, it is hoped, will bring democracy to South Africa. At the time of writing, Mandela, like all other black people in South Africa, still does not have the vote. The struggle is not yet resolved; the time and the lives it will take still unknown.

Whatever the ultimate cost, democratic rule must inevitably result in African control of the Republic, and this would be of great symbolic significance to black people all over the world. It would mean that the African continent was, once more, under the control of its indigenous population — free of foreign occupation and political control. Black South Africans would be as free and, in some cases, freer than many in the disapora. The struggles that have taken place for the abolition of slavery and, later for human rights in the West will in turn help to liberate Africa from its domination by Europeans.

Not all problems for African people in South Africa or throughout the world will be resolved, however. The countries of the continent are still controlled by foreign investments and unfavourable trading terms. They are still associated with poverty, disease and famine, political instability and corruption. In the cities of Europe and the Americas, areas occupied by black people are still identified with poverty, educational underachievement, unemployment, drugs and crime. But in the search for a common identity, national boundaries are losing some of their significance. Black people in the United States no longer think of themselves as Negroes or Blacks but as African-Americans. In Europe, Jamaicans, Barbadians, Nigerians, Trinidadians and Ghanaians are more eager to recognise their common roots. Africans of the diaspora no longer feel a sense of shame (or superiority) in identifying with Africa. In emotional terms, they are returning home.

That this is so indicates the level which has been reached in the reconstruction of the black image. The foundations had been laid by those who refused to accept the condition of slavery as permanent, and who worked, fought or escaped in attempts to change it. Before and since abolition, millions of black people struggled to maintain their own dignity and supported others in doing so.

Before Marcus Garvey, black leaders and achievers directed their energies to opposing the false images constructed over three centuries, seeking only their rightful recognition and understanding. Politically they requested their freedom. In recent decades, however, reconstruction has taken the form of asserting and demanding rights. Where rights are refused, they are gained through struggle.

In the intellectual arena, scholars have been researching and reasserting the history of Africa and Africans. Scientist, physicians, lawyers and other professional people make their contributions. Writers, poets, and performers and artists of every kind present their skills and creations to the world. It's significant and also symbolic that in Zimbabwe, where the European settlers once denied the creative ability of the Africans to construct the walls and towers of the old city (Section 1,12), Shona sculptors are now recognised as among the worlds finest artists. The present book adds only a few facets to the process, throwing light onto some obscure corners and attempting to bring together scattered areas of knowledge that demonstrate how the Reconstruction of the Black Image is based on solid — if sometimes concealed — foundations.

RECONSTRUCTING THE BLACK IMAGE in the HISTORY NATIONAL CURRICULUM

Key Stage 3: Core study unit I: The Roman Empire.

Unit 1. This book shows how Rome, a creative centre of classical Mediterranean culture, radiated its influence as far as West Africa. Pupils can see how its traditions remained among the Yoruba after the Muslim occupation of North Africa cut Africa off from the ancient cultures.

Africa was important in the history of Rome, starting with the struggle for supremacy between Rome and Carthage and the Punic Wars. Section II deals with the expedition of Hannibal from Africa across sea and mountains to Northern Italy. North Africa was an important Roman province, both for military purposes and for trade. Personnel were recruited from North Africa for the Roman army even before the Romans expanded their empire northwards into Europe (Section II).

Africa also contributed powerfully to the religious life of the Romans. Section III provides information on one Egyptian religion, the worship of Isis, practised in Rome prior to Christianity. During the Early Christian era, North Africa was one of the main centres of Christianity, and many of the early saints and bishops were natives of the region. It remained an important Christian centre until it was separated by the Donatist schism — and later conquered by the Muslim incursion.

Key Stage 3: Unit 11. Medieval Realms: British 1066 to 1500

The Norman rulers perceived themselves as part of Christendom. The high-handed action of Richard 1 of collecting money from Jewish merchants to finance the Crusades led indirectly to the first persecution of Jews in Britain.

This book considers how Britain, as part of Christendom, benefited from the learning accumulated in Muslim Spain and the role of that learning in triggering the Renaissance.

Key Stage 3: Unit 3. The making of the United Kingdom: Crowns, Parliament and people.

Section I of the present book deals with changes in Britain and Europe that resulted from the occupation of the Americas and the West African Slave Trade,.

Section II considers the historic relationships between the United Kingdom and the countries of Africa, the African people of the diaspora established by colonial slavery, and records the presence of African people in Britain from the end of the 17th century to the middle of the 19th. It also examines attitudes of the established Churches (Churches of England and Roman Catholic) towards slavery and compares these views with those held among non-conformist sects.

Section II also explores the changes in Britain resulting from the increased wealth brought in from the colonies: changes in architecture, increased scholarship and creativity, and the wealth to power the Industrial Revolution.

Key Stage 3: Unit 4. Expansion, trade and industry: Britain 1750 to 1900

British attitudes and perceptions of their former slaves and other colonial and foreign peoples are considered in Section I, during the occupation of the New World, after the abolition of slavery and during Colonial expansion, and the ways that these attitudes and perceptions affected the colonised people are discussed.

Section II takes these themes further, particularly into areas of resistance, conflict and interaction. It illustrates incidences of co-operation between colonisers and colonised in external conflicts and draws parallels between the struggles for abolition and for political and social reform in Britain.

Section III considers the influence of colonial people on popular culture.

Section IV deals with the struggle of colonial people for political independence and considers some of those societies as they existed before colonisation.

Key Stage 3: Unit 5. The era of the Second World War.

Section II of this book considers the role of colonial people in the major wars of the 20th century. It explores later conflicts with special reference to African people in the diaspora and in Africa itself. The migrations of African people into European countries is set in its historical context.

Supplementary Study Unit in the National Curriculum

Reconstructing the Black Image is particularly relevant to the following:

Britain and the American revolution.
The British Empire and its impact in the last quarter of the nineteenth century.
Britain and the Great War 1914 to 1918.
The Crusades
The past societies of Africa and America
Also Examples 1, 5, and 6.

PICTURE CREDITS AND ACKNOWLEDGEMENTS

Section I

1,5,8	Courtesy of the British Museum, London
2	By permission of Nigeria's Honourable Secretary for Information and Culture
3	Painting by Roger van der Weyden; courtesy of the Kaiser Friederich Museum, Berlin
4	Courtesy of the Bibliotheque Nationale, Paris
7	Olfert, D: *Description de l'Afrique*, Amsterdam, 1685
11	*Sunday Times Magazine,* Nov 21, 1971
12	Courtesy of the National Archive, Zimbabwe

Section II

3	Collection; the Royal Albert Museum (Exeter Museums and Art Gallery)
4, 11	Courtesy of the British Museum, London
5	Courtesy of the Imperial War Museum, London
6	Courtesy of the Bibliotheque Nationale, Paris
7	By permission of the Museum of Fine Arts, Budapest
8	(and cover) Fresco in the Church of San Francisco, Arezzo
9	By permission of the Royal Collection
10	**Victory of Alexander over Darius**, Museo Archeologico, Naples

Section III

1	*Ebony* December 1975
5	*Mind Alive* Vol.2, No.7, Marshall Cavendish, 1968
6	By permission of the Houghton Library, Harvard University
7	Courtesy of Alte Alte Pinakothek, Munich
8	Chapel of San Giorgio, Basilica of Sant' Antonio, Padua, Courtesy the Soprintendente
9	The Imperial Villa, Pompei, Courtesy the Soprintendente

10,12,15	Courtesy of the National Museum, Cairo
14	*West Indian World* Sept 8, 1978

Section IV

1	Courtesy of Garvey Rodney Visual Archives
2	*Ebony* February 1969
3	*The Autobiography of Kwame Nkrumah,* Allen and Unwin, 1957
4,12	from Barth, H: *Travels and discoveries in North and Central Africa* London, 1875
5,7,9	Courtesy of the National Museum, Cairo
8	Alfred, C: *The Egyptians* Thames and Hudson, 1987
10	Fage, J.D: *A History of Africa* Hutchinson Africa Series, 1958 (permission of Routledge)
11	Courtesy of the National Archive, Zimbabwe
14	Courtesy of the Museum of Mankind, London
15	Painting by Albert Eckhout, National Museum of Denmark
16	Isaacs, N: *Travels and Adventures in Eastern Africa* London, 1836
17	Stanley, H.M. *How I found Livingstone* London 1873
18	Courtesy of Central Press, London
19	By permission of the Government of Zimbabwe
20	Courtesy of British Defence and Aid Fund for Southern Africa

[All other paintings, drawings, photographs by the author]

Every effort has been made to reach copyright holders. The publishers would be glad to hear from anyone whose rights they have unknowingly infringed.

Bibliography

Arrian — *The Campaigns of Alexander.* Penguin Books England, 1971

Barclay-Lloyd, Joan. *African Animals In Renaissance Art and Literature.* Oxford, Clarendon Press, 1971.

Bovill, E.W. *The Golden Trade of the Moors.* Oxford University Press 1966.

Chamberlin, Russell. *Loot!* Thames and Hudson 1983.

Crowder, Michael. The Impact of Two World Wars on Africa. *History Today* Vol.34, January, 1984.

Davidson, Basil. *The African Past: Chronicles from Antiquity to Modern Times.* Longmans, Green & Co, 1964.

Guide to African History. Elephant Books, 1963

The Story of Africa. Mitchell Beazley — A Channel Four Book, 1980

de Garmont, Sancho. *The Strong Brown God.* Hart Davis Mc Gibbon, 1975

Dobler, Laninia. *When Greatness Called.* Noble and Noble Publishers, New York, 1970

Drower, Margaret. *Nubia, the Drowning Land.* Longmans Young Books, 1970

Gillon, Werner. *A Short History of African Art.* Viking Penguin Books, 1986

Greenwood, R. & Hamber, S. *Arawaks to Africans.* Caribbean Certificate History. McMillan Caribbean, 1979

Husband, Charles. *Race in Britain,* Hutchinson, 1987

Jordan, Paul. *Egypt, the Black Land,* 1976 Phaidon

Little, Kenneth. *Negroes in Britain.* R. Kegan Paul, 1947

Lommel, Andreas. *Prehistoric and Primitive Man.* Paul Hamlyn 1966

Magnusson, Magnus. 'The Builders of Zimbabwe' in *Discovery of Lost World.* Edited by J. Thorndike Jr. New York American Heritage Publication, 1979

Peck, William, H. *Drawings From Ancient Egypt.* Thames and Hudson, 1978

Read, Jan. *The Moors in Spain and Portugal.* Faber and Faber, 1974

Robert, Brian. *The Zulu Kings* Hamish Hamilton, 1974

Roper, H.T. *The Rise of Christian Europe*. Thames and Hudson, 1965

Rogers, J.A. *Sex and Race Part 1* New York, Helga M. Rogers, 1952

100 Amazing Facts About The Negro. Helga M. Rogers, 1957

Shyllon, Florian. *Black People in Britain 1555-1833,* Oxford University Press, 1977

Snowden, Frank M. Jr. *Blacks in Antiquity.* Massachusetts The Belknap Press, 1972

Tannahill, Reay. *Sex in History.* Hamish Hamilton, 1980

Thompson, Dorothy. *The Early Chartists.* MacMillan, 1971

Wellard, James. *Lost Worlds Of Africa.* Hutchinson, 1967

Williams, Eric. *From Columbus to Castro. The History of The Caribbean 1492-1959.* Deutsch, 1984

Woodward, E.G. *The Age Of Reform.* Clarendon Press, 1938

The above list is by no means a complete bibliography. The research which led to this work was carried out over several years and at several locations, mainly at Springfield, in Kent. The list provided represents those sources recorded by the author and only those accessible at the time of writing.

Other authors I should like to acknowledge for their influence on my work are: J.L. Benson, John Boardman, Christine Bolt, Christopher Bradford, Harry Carter, Kenneth Clarke, Lewis P. Curtis, J.D. Fage, Bamber Gascoine, Michael Grant, D.A. Lorimer, R.A. Markus, Joshua Prawer, and Desmond Stewart.

References

SECTION ONE

1. Lommel, A., 1966
2. ibid
3. Bovill, E.W., 1966
4. Greenwood, R. & Hamber, S., 1979
5. Tannahill. R., 1980
6. Davidson, B., 1980
7. Barclay-Floyd, J., 1971
8. Davidson, B., 1963
9. Magnusson, M., 1979
10. Greenwood, R. & Hamber, S., 1979
11. ibid
12. Rogers, J.A., 1952
13. de Garmont, S., 1975
14. Davidson, B., 1963
15. Williams, E., 1984
16. ibid
17. Lommel, A., 1966
18. ibid
19. Jordan, P., 1976
20. Drower, M., 1970
21. Peck, W.H., 1978
22. Drower, M., 1970
23. ibid
24. Davidson, B., 1964
25. ibid
26. ibid
27. ibid
28. Rogers, J.A., 1952
29. Snowden F.M., 1972
30. Bovill, E.W., 1966
31. ibid
32. Bovill, W., 1966
33. Roberts, 1974

SECTION TWO

1. Davidson, B., 1963
2. Davidson, B., 1980
3. ibid
4. Davidson, B., 1964
5. Williams, E., 1984
6. ibid
7. ibid
8. ibid
9. Little.
10. Woodward, E.L., 1938
11. Thompson, D., 1971
12. The Grenada Handbook 1946
13. Husband, C., 1987
14. Dobler, L., 1970
15. ibid
16. ibid
17. ibid
18. Davidson, 1964
19. Wellard, J., 1967
20. Read, J., 1974
21. ibid
22. Roper, H.T.
23. Bovill, E.W., 1966
24. Snowden, R.M., 1972
25. Bovill, E.W., 1966
26. Arrian, 1971
27. Drower, M., 1970

SECTION THREE

1. Shyllon, F., 1977
2. Davidson, B., 1980
3. Drower, M., 1970
4. Rogers, J.A., 1957
5. Mind Alive Series: The Marshall Cavendish Encyclopaedia Vol.1, No.5.
6. The Holy Bible Jeremiah 44
7. Mind Alive Series
8. The Unexplained Mysteries of Mind Space and Time Vol.4.
9. Rogers, J.A., 1952
10. Read, J., 1974

SECTION FOUR

1. Capital Issues Supplement August 1987, London Strategic Policy Unit.
2. Davidson, B., 1980
3. Jordan, P., 1976
4. Drower, M., 1970
5. Jordan, P. 1976
6. Davidson, B., 1964
7. Bovill, E.W., 1966
8. Davidson, B., 1980
9. Chamberlin LOOT!, 1983
10. Gillon, W.
11. The British Empire - Time Life Book No84, 1973
12. Robert, B., 1974
13. Davidson, B., 1980
14. ibid

KIDNEY CANCER

Cancer Treatment and Research

Steven T. Rosen, M.D., *Series Editor*

Goldstein, L.J., Ozols, R.F. (eds): *Anticancer Drug Resistance. Advances in Molecular and Clinical Research.* 1994. ISBN 0-7923-2836-1.
Hong, W.K., Weber, R.S. (eds): *Head and Neck Cancer. Basic and Clinical Aspects.* 1994. ISBN 0-7923-3015-3.
Thall, P.F. (ed.): *Recent Advances in Clinical Trial Design and Analysis.* 1995. ISBN 0-7923-3235-0.
Buckner, C.D. (ed.): *Technical and Biological Components of Marrow Transplantation.* 1995. ISBN 0-7923-3394-2.
Winter, J.N. (ed.): *Blood Stem Cell Transplantation.* 1997. ISBN 0-7923-4260-7.
Muggia, F.M. (ed.): *Concepts, Mechanisms, and New Targets for Chemotherapy.* 1995. ISBN 0-7923-3525-2.
Klastersky, J. (ed.): *Infectious Complications of Cancer.* 1995. ISBN 0-7923-3598-8.
Kurzrock, R., Talpaz, M. (eds): *Cytokines: Interleukins and Their Receptors.* 1995. ISBN 0-7923-3636-4.
Sugarbaker, P. (ed.): *Peritoneal Carcinomatosis: Drugs and Diseases.* 1995. ISBN 0-7923-3726-3.
Sugarbaker, P. (ed.): *Peritoneal Carcinomatosis: Principles of Management.* 1995. ISBN 0-7923-3727-1.
Dickson, R.B., Lippman, M.E. (eds): *Mammary Tumor Cell Cycle, Differentiation and Metastasis.* 1995. ISBN 0-7923-3905-3.
Freireich, E.J., Kantarjian, H. (eds): *Molecular Genetics and Therapy of Leukemia.* 1995. ISBN 0-7923-3912-6.
Cabanillas, F., Rodriguez, M.A. (eds): *Advances in Lymphoma Research.* 1996. ISBN 0-7923-3929-0.
Miller, A.B. (ed.): *Advances in Cancer Screening.* 1996. ISBN 0-7923-4019-1.
Hait , W.N. (ed.): *Drug Resistance.* 1996. ISBN 0-7923-4022-1.
Pienta, K.J. (ed.): *Diagnosis and Treatment of Genitourinary Malignancies.* 1996. ISBN 0-7923-4164-3.
Arnold, A.J. (ed.): *Endocrine Neoplasms.* 1997. ISBN 0-7923-4354-9.
Pollock, R.E. (ed.): *Surgical Oncology.* 1997. ISBN 0-7923-9900-5.
Verweij, J., Pinedo, H.M., Suit, H.D. (eds): *Soft Tissue Sarcomas: Present Achievements and Future Prospects.* 1997. ISBN 0-7923-9913-7.
Walterhouse, D.O., Cohn, S.L. (eds): *Diagnostic and Therapeutic Advances in Pediatric Oncology.* 1997. ISBN 0-7923-9978-1.
Mittal, B.B., Purdy, J.A., Ang, K.K. (eds): *Radiation Therapy.* 1998. ISBN 0-7923-9981-1.
Foon, K.A., Muss, H.B. (eds): *Biological and Hormonal Therapies of Cancer.* 1998. ISBN 0-7923-9997-8.
Ozols, R.F. (ed.): *Gynecologic Oncology.* 1998. ISBN 0-7923-8070-3.
Noskin, G.A. (ed.): *Management of Infectious Complications in Cancer Patients.* 1998. ISBN 0-7923-8150-5.
Bennett, C.L. (ed.): *Cancer Policy.* 1998. ISBN 0-7923-8203-X.
Benson, A.B. (ed.): *Gastrointestinal Oncology.* 1998. ISBN 0-7923-8205-6.
Tallman, M.S., Gordon, L.I. (eds): *Diagnostic and Therapeutic Advances in Hematologic Malignancies.* 1998. ISBN 0-7923-8206-4.
von Gunten, C.F. (ed.): *Palliative Care and Rehabilitation of Cancer Patients.* 1999. ISBN 0-7923-8525-X.
Burt, R.K., Brush, M.M. (eds): *Advances in Allogeneic Hematopoietic Stem Cell Transplantation.* 1999. ISBN 0-7923-7714-1.
Angelos, P. (ed.): *Ethical Issues in Cancer Patient Care* 2000. ISBN 0-7923-7726-5.
Gradishar, W.J., Wood, W.C. (eds): *Advances in Breast Cancer Management.* 2000. ISBN 0-7923-7890-3.
Sparano, Joseph A. (ed.): *HIV & HTLV-I Associated Malignancies.* 2001. ISBN 0-7923-7220-4.
Ettinger, David S. (ed.): *Thoracic Oncology.* 2001. ISBN 0-7923-7248-4.
Bergan, Raymond C. (ed.): *Cancer Chemoprevention.* 2001. ISBN 0-7923-7259-X.
Raza, A., Mundle, S.D. (eds): *Myelodysplastic Syndromes & Secondary Acute Myelogenous Leukemia.* 2001. ISBN 0-7923-7396.
Talamonti, Mark S. (ed.): *Liver Directed Therapy for Primary and Metastatic Liver Tumors.* 2001. ISBN 0-7923-7523-8.
Stack, M.S., Fishman, D.A. (eds): *Ovarian Cancer.* 2001. ISBN 0-7923-7530-0.
Bashey, A., Ball, E.D. (eds): *Non-Myeloablative Allogeneic Transplantation.* 2002. ISBN 0-7923-7646-3.
Leong, Stanley P.L. (ed.): *Atlas of Selective Sentinel Lymphadenectomy for Melanoma, Breast Cancer and Colon Cancer.* 2002. ISBN 1-4020-7013-6.
Andersson, B., Murray D. (eds): *Clinically Relevant Resistance in Cancer Chemotherapy.* 2002. ISBN 1-4020-7200-7.
Beam, C. (ed.): *Biostatistical Applications in Cancer Research.* 2002. ISBN 1-4020-7226-0.
Brockstein, B., Masters, G. (eds): *Head and Neck Cancer.* 2003. ISBN 1-4020-7336-4.
Frank, D.A. (ed.): *Signal Transduction in Cancer.* 2003. ISBN 1-4020-7340-2.
Figlin, Robert A. (ed.): *Kidney Cancer.* 2003. ISBN 1-4020-7457-3.

KIDNEY CANCER

Edited by
ROBERT A. FIGLIN
University of California, Los Angeles, CA

KLUWER ACADEMIC PUBLISHERS
BOSTON / DORDRECHT / LONDON

Distributors for North, Central and South America:
Kluwer Academic Publishers
101 Philip Drive
Assinippi Park
Norwell, Massachusetts 02061 USA
Telephone (781) 871-6600
Fax (781) 681-9045
E-Mail: kluwer@wkap.com

Distributors for all other countries:
Kluwer Academic Publishers Group
Post Office Box 322
3300 AH Dordrecht, THE NETHERLANDS
Telephone 31 786 576 000
Fax 31 786 576 254
E-Mail: services@wkap.nl

 Electronic Services <http://www.wkap.nl>

Library of Congress Cataloging-in-Publication Data

Kidney cancer / edited by Robert A. Figlin
    p. ; cm. – (Cancer treatment and research ; 116)
  Includes bibliographical references and index.
  ISBN 1-4020-7457-3 (alk. paper)
  1. Kidneys--Cancer. I. Figlin, Robert A. II. Series.
  [DNLM: 1. Kidney Neoplasms--surgery. 2. Carcinoma, Renal Cell--immunology.
3. Carcinoma, Renal Cell--therapy. 4. Kidney Neoplasms--immunology. WJ 368
K453 2003]
RC280.K5K527 2003
616.99'461--dc21   2003051644

Printed on acid-free paper.
Printed in the United States of America.

*The Publisher offers discounts on this book for course use and bulk purchases.
For further information, send email to <Laura.Walsh@wkap.com>.*

TABLE OF CONTENTS

ROBERT A. FIGLIN, M.D., F.A.C.P.

In Kidney Cancer, authoritative authors address the diverse questions facing the clinical and research community in this interesting disease. This book is directed at clinicians and scientists both basic and clinical, whose areas of expertise encompass renal cell carcinoma. Renal cell carcinoma is a heterogeneous disease. We are now coming to understand that it has not only different pathological findings, but more importantly different genetic patterns. In addressing the molecular genetics of kidney cancer we are better able to understand the potential future targets for therapy. With the recent advances in database technology, including tissue arrays, there are now well established criteria to predict survival in patients that present with renal cell carcinoma. These new and improved algorithms for staging and prognosis, help us identify populations at risk with resected and metastatic renal cell carcinoma. These findings enable us to direct patient specific therapy both in the clinic and from the research community, and establishes the eligibility criteria for future clinical trials.

Surgical approaches in renal cell carcinoma continue to evolve. Not only do we finally understand that radical nephrectomy in selected patients with metastatic disease, when followed by immune based treatment improves survival, but we now have a large body of data supporting both nephron sparing surgery, as well as laproscopic radical nephrectomy, and the burgeoning area of minimally invasive surgery. As with breast cancer treatment several decades ago, we now understand that preserving renal function can be accomplished while optimizing cancer care.

The systemic therapies of renal cell carcinoma remain immunologically based.

Interleukin-2 is the only FDA approved treatment for metastatic renal cell carcinoma, and recent evidence suggests that high dose interleukin-2 is the treatment of choice for selected patients. The role of systemic therapy continues to evolve, but we have yet not found cytotoxic agents capable of producing clinically important remissions in renal cell carcinoma. Current and future efforts in cell, gene and vaccine based therapy, as well as, antibodies directed at specific targets are the methods currently in the clinical research arena that continue to support the immunologic basis of renal cell carcinoma. The ground breaking work of the National Cancer Institute demonstrating that mini allo transplantation can benefit selected populations of patients with renal cell carcinoma, demonstrates the continued growth and connection between understanding the host and the tumor in this patient population.

Lastly, new strategies in renal cell carcinoma must be developed. These can only be developed with a better understanding of the targets associated with cancer cell growth, that then enable translational research scientists to target specific genetic and phenotypic alterations that allow for more specific cancer therapy.

Renal cell carcinoma remains a prototype cancer. It is a cancer that requires an integrative approach, has a well defined and understood genetic predisposition that requires a firm understanding of the biology and clinical behavior, the appropriate and important role of surgery, and the ever expanding role of immunologic manipulation and target specific treatment. I hope the readers appreciate the efforts by the authors in this book, who continue to demonstrate and commit themselves to this research effort.